THE COVERING

JAY STRACK

AND

HANK HANEGRAAFF

NELSON IMPACT
A Division of Thomas Nelson Publishers
Since 1798

www.thomasnelson.com

Published by Nelson Impact, a Division of Thomas Nelson, Inc., P.O. Box 141000, Nashville, TN 37214.

ISBN: 1-4185-0600-1

Printed in the United States of America

06 07 08 09 RRD 9 8 7 6 5 4 3 2 1

Page design by Crosslin Creative
2743 Douglas Lane, Thompsons Station, Tennessee 37179

CONTENTS

INTRODUCTION

Did you know that you are in a war engaged against an invisible enemy? In fact, we all are. We can't see it or touch it, but it's there. It approaches you on the Internet, in the hall at school, on the television screen. The enemy is Satan, the devil, and he is real and powerful. But the good news of the Bible is that we have the "covering"—the full armor of God—an impenetrable barrier against which the fiery darts of the evil one are powerless.

One of the most inescapable realities of the Christian worldview is that "we do not wrestle against flesh and blood, but against principalities, against powers, against the rulers of the darkness of this age, against spiritual hosts of wickedness in the heavenly places" (Ephesians 6:12). Amazon.com now lists more than 500 titles on spiritual warfare, and Google displays over 1,000,000 references to "Christian spiritual warfare". It appears that people everywhere are thinking a great deal about spiritual warfare these days. The good news is that God has a plan to protect you from evil in the spiritual battles in your life.

Adapted from the highly regarded book, *The Covering*, this study guide explains that we dare not overestimate the power of the devil, and God has given us the tools for victory. In this 8-week study, you will learn how to put on the full armor of God so that you will be intimately acquainted with each piece of the armor and its effectiveness in your life. The victory is yours for the taking!

> *Finally, be strong in the Lord and in*
> *his mighty power. Put on the full armor of God*
> *so that you can take your stand against the*
> *devil's schemes. For our struggle is not against*
> *flesh and blood, but against the rulers,*
> *against the authorities, against the powers of*
> *this dark world and against the spiritual*
> *forces of evil in the heavenly realms. Therefore*
> *put on the full armor of God, so that when*
> *the day of evil comes, you may be able to*
> *stand your ground, and after you have done*

everything, to stand. Stand firm then, with
the belt of truth buckled around your waist,
with the breastplate of righteousness in place,
and with your feet fitted with the readiness that
comes from the gospel of peace. In addition
to all this, take up the shield of faith,
with which you can extinguish all the
flaming arrows of the evil one. Take the
helmet of salvation and the sword of
the Spirit, which is the word of God.

—Ephesians 6:10–17 (NIV)

KEY

STUDENT LEADERSHIP UNIVERSITY CURRICULUM

Throughout this study guide, you will see several icons or headings that represent an idea, a statement, or a question that we want you to consider as you experience Scripture in this study guide series. Refer to the descriptions below to help you remember what the icons and headings mean.

transfuse (trans FYOOZ)˙: to cause to pass from one to another; transmit

The goal of the lesson for the week.

Experience Scripture: Learning to really experience Scripture is the key element to "getting" who God is and all that He has in store for you.

infuse (in FYOOZ)˙: to cause to be permeated with something (as a principle or quality) that alters usually for the better

Through journaling, group discussion, and personal study, experience Scripture as it permeates your heart and alters your life.

 Future Tense Living: Your choices today will determine your future. Learn how to live with dynamic purpose and influence.

 Attitude Reloaded: Rethink your attitude! Learn to replace self-centered, negative, or limited thoughts

with positive, courageous, compassionate thoughts that are based on God's unlimited ability and power.

 In His Steps: Every attitude and action of your life should begin with the questions, How would Jesus respond to this person and situation before me? What would He choose to do?

diffuse (di FYOOZ); to pour out and permit or cause to spread freely; to extend, scatter

Once God's Word is infused into your heart, it will pour forth to others without restraint. In this section, explore what that looks like in your daily life.

 Called to Lead: Learn how to lead others as Christ would.

Called to Stand: Know what you believe and learn how to defend it with clarity and strength.

Called to Share: Sharing truth and serving others are results of a transformed life. How can you share with others the awesome things you're learning?

One Thing: Consider ONE THING you can do this week to make a difference in your life and/or the life of another.

FUSE BOX

Power up for the week with this focused truth.

CHAPTER 1

CAN THE DEVIL MAKE YOU DO IT?

KEY SCRIPTURE

Finally, my brethren, be strong in the Lord and in the power of His might. Put on the whole armor of God, that you may be able to stand against the wiles of the devil.
—Ephesians 6:10–11

WHY KNOW IT?

✦ 59% of people currently believe that "Satan is not a living being but is just a symbol of evil."[1]

✦ A recent Gallup survey shows that just about three in four Americans hold some paranormal belief. There are no significant differences in belief by age, gender, education, or region of the country.[2]

transfuse (trans FYOOZ): to cause to pass from one to another; transmit

America's fascination with the supernatural is ever-growing as evidenced by the immense popularity of TV shows, movies, and video games such as:

TV: *Charmed, The Ghost Whisperer, Point Pleasant, Supernatural, Medium*

MOVIES: *The Exorcism of Emily Rose, The Exorcist, The Sixth Sense, The Grudge*

VIDEO GAMES: *The Suffering, Temujin: A Supernatural Adventure, Fatal Frame III, Phantom Dust*

And the list goes on. . . .

Far from falling out of style, TV shows, video games, and movies that deal with the supernatural are becoming increasingly popular. For many people, Satan and demonic powers have become a source of entertainment rather than a reality spoken of in the Bible. The excuse, "The devil made me do it!" was first coined by a comedian some thirty years ago, and it has continued to be used as a comedic cop-out that is anything but funny.

Make no mistake: Satan is real. But how do you overcome him? How do you make the right choices?

✦ 47% of young people cite that attending church does not give them enough understanding of the Bible to base all their decisions on biblical principles.[4]

The Bible emphatically warns that there is warfare against the wicked ones—namely, Satan and his demons. The purpose of this study guide, *The Covering,* is to show you that the key to victory in the invisible war with Satan is found in consistent discipleship and not in instant "deliverance" claims.

The "covering" described in Scripture is the full armor of God found in Ephesians 6. It is an impenetrable barrier against which the fiery darts of the evil one are impotent. When we are clothed in the covering, we are invincible. When we are not clothed in the armor of God, we are pawns in the devil's evil schemes.

The greatest trick the devil ever pulled was convincing the world he didn't exist.

—Roger "Verbal" Kint,
The Usual Suspects[3]

For your obedience has become known to all.
Therefore I am glad on your behalf; but I want
you to be wise in what is good, and simple
[innocent] concerning evil. —**Romans 16:19**

Is it dangerous to study about Satan? Some people believe that by informing students about these issues, we are exposing them to spiritual danger. Such a view is willingly ignorant of what is plainly taught in Scripture and of what is happening in today's culture. Scripture teaches the reality of Satan but discourages fascination with or worship of him; it assures us of Jesus's victory over Satan and discourages fear of him.

> Keep your study in the truth of God's Word and not in the imagination of man. In this way, you will find truth and strength instead of lies and fear.

In his classic *The Screwtape Letters,* C. S. Lewis talks of the devil: "There are two equal and opposite errors into which our race can fall about the devils [demons]. One is to disbelieve in their existence. The other is to believe, and to feel an unhealthy interest in them. They themselves are equally pleased by both errors and hail a materialist or a magician with the same delight."[5]

GROUP DISCUSSION

✦ Do you think that movies and TV give an accurate picture of who Satan is?

No. They depict him as a villian that wants to be seen.

✦ Do you believe that Satan is real?

Yes, and I will admit I have felt him in me

✦ Is Satan powerful?

Yes, He was God's right hand man. So He had power

✦ Is it dangerous to study about Satan? Why or why not?

Both you learn about him which He wants. But you must know your enemy to beat them

The New Testament repeatedly affirms the reality of both demons and a personal, malignant being who is referred to by various names: Satan, the serpent, and the devil, to name a few. But while the Bible does present Satan and demons as powerful spiritual beings, God's Word is also clear that Satan is no match for God.

A central message of both the Old and New Testaments is God's triumph over the evil one. First John 3:8 says, "He who sins is of the devil, for the devil has sinned from the beginning. For this purpose the Son of God was manifested, that He might destroy the works of the devil."

To illustrate God's rule and reign and how that translates into victory for His children in spiritual warfare, let's deal head-on with one of the questions about demons that Christian teenagers often ask.

infuse (in FYOOZ)*;* to cause to be permeated with something (as a principle or quality) that alters usually for the better

Can Christians Be Possessed or Inhabited by Demons?
For the answer to this question, let's go straight to the words of Christ Himself: "How can one enter a strong man's house and plunder his goods, unless he first binds the strong man?" (Matthew 12:29).

Who is "the strong man"?

✦ To a demon-possessed person—the *strong man* is the devil.

✦ To a Spirit-indwelt believer—the strong man is God.

Christ asks a straightforward question, one that concludes with an obvious answer. In order for demons to possess believers, they first have to bind the *strong man* who occupies them—namely, Christ Himself!

✦ Then He explains, "When an unclean spirit goes out of a man, he goes through dry places, seeking rest, and finds none. Then he says, 'I will return to my house from which I came.' And when he comes, he finds it empty, swept, and put in order. Then he goes and takes with him seven other spirits more wicked than himself, and they enter and dwell there; and the last state of that man is worse than the first" (Matthew 12:43–45).

Once again, Jesus teaches with precision and leaves us no guesswork.

✦ If we are unoccupied by the Holy Spirit, we subject ourselves to the possibility of being inhabited by demons.

✦ If our house (a body/soul unity) is Christ's home, then the devil finds no place to dwell in us.

Let's look at a few other Scriptures:

✦ "Jesus answered and said to him, 'If anyone loves Me, he will keep My word; and My Father will love him, and We will come to him and make Our home with him'" (John 14:23).

✦ "But you are not in the flesh but in the Spirit, if indeed the Spirit of God dwells in you. Now if anyone does not have the Spirit of Christ, he is not His" (Romans 8:9).

✦ "But if the Spirit of Him who raised Jesus from the dead dwells in you, He who raised Christ from the dead will also give life to your mortal bodies through His Spirit who dwells in you" (Romans 8:11).

The consistent teaching of Scripture is that Christians cannot be controlled against their wills through demonic inhabitation. The principle is foolproof. If you are a follower of Christ, the King Himself dwells in you.

Is it possible that your lack of faith in God's power over Satan in your life is rooted in a disobedience to God's Word?

Yes Satan can't come into your life unless you sin

To love Jesus is to obey Him. Commit to living out your love for Christ by filling in the blanks with five specific choices you can make to obey Christ this week:

Because I love Him, I will <u>work harder</u>.

Because I love Him, I will <u>be more respectful</u>.

Because I love Him, I will <u>be nicer to my sister</u>.

Because I love Him, I will <u>not get as deppressed with morga</u>

Because I love Him, I will <u>trust him</u>.

What is ONE THING you can change about the choices you are making this week that will help you to love and obey Christ?

trust him that He will lead me to a path of good and great Things.

We have looked at specific teachings of Christ. These alone are enough to confirm that Satan cannot live where Christ rules. But for the skeptic, there is still more!

Rest yourself completely assured with this statement: "You are of God, little children, and have overcome them, because He who is in you is greater than he who is in the world" (1 John 4:4).

Are you looking for strength in daily living? Remember and rehearse 1 John 4:4. No dispute—no argument—no worries:

Greater is He [the Holy Spirit] *who lives in* _____
___Strider___ [your name] *than he* [the devil] *who is in the world.*

To deny the truth of these scriptures because of some people's alleged experiences or stories is to greatly overestimate the power and realm of Satan.

diffuse (di FYOOZ): to pour out and permit or cause to spread freely; to extend, scatter

There are two common misunderstandings that appear to give Satan more power than he truthfully has. These must be examined in the light of Scripture.

Healing the Body Is Not the Same As Casting Out Demons

Some people say that every illness is caused by a demon. Therefore, they proclaim that every healing of the body is in reality an exorcism. Get this: Jesus *did not* teach that *anywhere!*

✦ *Jesus spoke of divine healing as the opportunity to show the glory of God.* In John 9:2–3, His disciples asked Him, "Rabbi, who sinned, this man or his parents, that he was born blind?" Jesus answered,

"Neither this man nor his parents sinned, but that the works of God should be revealed in him."

✦ *Jesus spoke separately of casting out unclean spirits and of healing disease.* "When He had called His twelve disciples to Him, He gave them power over unclean spirits, to cast them out, and to heal all kinds of sickness and all kinds of disease" (Matthew 10:1).

✦ *Jesus's acts of healing lacked all the common features of an exorcism account.* "Now He was teaching in one of the synagogues on the Sabbath. And behold, there was a woman who had a spirit of infirmity eighteen years, and was bent over and could in no way raise herself up. But when Jesus saw her, He called her to Him and said to her, 'Woman, you are loosed from your infirmity.' And He laid His hands on her, and immediately she was made straight, and glorified God. But the ruler of the synagogue answered with indignation, because Jesus had healed on the Sabbath" (Luke 13:10–14).

> According to Jesus, *love* equals *obedience:*
>
> "If anyone loves Me, he will keep My word; and My Father will love him, and We will come to him and make Our home with him" (John 14:23; emphasis added).

Note:

✦ Jesus addressed the woman rather than addressing a demon;

✦ Satan did not speak through the crippled woman;

✦ the synagogue ruler referred to the instance as a healing and not an exorcism;

+ being *in the synagogue* is not synonymous with being an indwelt believer. Christ does refer to her as "a daughter of Abraham" (v. 16), but not all descendants of Abraham have the faith of Abraham (Romans 9:7–8; Matthew 3:9).

The Devil Does Not Make Anyone Sin Against His or Her Will

The "devil made me do it" is little more than a convenient cop-out for sin. Satan can work to tempt you, but he cannot force you to act upon that temptation.

The Bible says, "Each one is tempted when he is drawn away by his own desires and enticed. Then, when desire has conceived, it gives birth to sin; and sin, when it is full-grown, brings forth death. Do not be deceived, my beloved brethren" (James 1:14–16).

+ *Jesus spoke of temptation and not demonization as the means by which Satan entices us.* He specifically taught the disciples to pray, "Do not lead us into temptation, but deliver us from the evil one" (Matthew 6:13).

+ *Jesus taught that the heart of man, not demon possession, is responsible for evil acts.* "For out of the heart proceed evil thoughts, murders, adulteries, fornications, thefts, false witness, blasphemies" (Matthew 15:19).

If you hear a story of a Christian who was supposedly indwelled by a demon, how would you lovingly correct the misunderstanding? List at least three reasons and give the Scripture reference for each:

1. _____

2. _____

3. _____

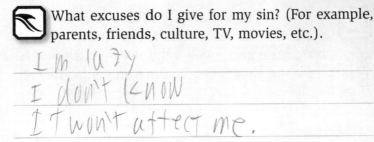

What excuses do I give for my sin? (For example, parents, friends, culture, TV, movies, etc.).

I'm lazy

I don't know

It won't affect me.

How does making excuses affect my ability to influence others?

We have thoroughly examined and understood that Satan cannot control you against your will. No Christian can be indwelled by him, but we are forewarned to "be sober, be vigilant; because your adversary the devil walks about like a roaring lion, seeking whom he may devour" (1 Peter 5:8). Satan is a roaring lion, but the length of his leash is determined by the Lord.

Satan wants nothing more than to destroy your testimony before others and to disrupt your fellowship with God. He cannot have you, but he can and will do whatever he can to keep you from bringing others to Christ. You must understand this.

Do visible, public stands for Christ make a strong impact on your school and your peers? (For example, a See You at the Pole rally, wearing a Christian T-shirt, carrying your Bible, inviting others to Christian clubs, etc.).

Nowadays no. Not really

In the next seven weeks, we will thoroughly examine every part of spiritual armor given to us by the Lord to soundly defeat Satan's attempts to stop our influence for the kingdom of God. For this reason, Paul urges us to "put on the whole armor of God, that you may be able to stand against the wiles [schemes] of the devil" (Ephesians 6:11).

It will be an amazing time in your life—one of testing, proving, and great victory.

FUSE BOX

To understand spiritual warfare and to overcome temptation, the Christian must focus on the power of God rather than on the schemes of the devil.

NOTES

> It is not the rule of Satan that a believer need be concerned with; it is the rule of one's own heart that must receive our full attention. Do not give Satan glory that he does not deserve.

PRIVATE WORLD DEVOTIONS

MONDAY: See it. Read the surrounding passages or chapter for the Key Scripture so that you can get an understanding of the background and context. This helps you to really *see* the verse.

TUESDAY: Hear it. Read the daily Key Scripture and/or surrounding passage out loud, putting your name in, if applicable. For example, <u>John</u> *can do all things through Christ. Thieves have come to destroy* <u>John</u>, *but Jesus has come that* <u>John</u> *might have eternal life.*

WEDNESDAY: Write it. Write the verse and then what it says about:

- ✦ *Others:* Respond, serve, and love as Jesus would.
- ✦ *Me:* Specific attitudes, choices, or habits.
- ✦ *God:* His love, mercy, holiness, peace, joy, etc.

PRIVATE WORLD JOURNAL

I am grateful for—I praise You for—I am feeling—I am thinking—I need help with

PRIVATE WORLD DEVOTIONS *(Continued)*

THURSDAY: Memorize it. Take the verse with you—write it on a card or put it in your phone, iPod, or PDA. Go over it throughout the day so that it begins to *live* in your heart and mind.

FRIDAY: Pray it. Personalize the verse as you pray for yourself or for others or in praise to God. To pray is literally "to think about." Try thinking out loud or writing in your **PRIVATE WORLD JOURNAL.**

SATURDAY: Share it. Ask the Lord to bring someone to mind or in your path today who needs good news. Don't be shy—just let it out! Whether you IM, write, text, tell, or send it, the joy of God's Word will flow from your heart into theirs.

PRAYER REQUESTS

Date	Name	Need	Answer

PRIVATE WORLD JOURNAL

I am grateful for—I praise You for—I am feeling—I am thinking—I need help with

NOTES

CHAPTER 2

THE BATTLE FOR YOUR MIND

KEY SCRIPTURE

For our struggle is not against flesh and blood, but against the rulers, against the authorities, against the powers of this dark world and against the spiritual forces of evil in the heavenly realms. Therefore put on the full armor of God so that when the day of evil comes, you may be able to stand your ground, and after you have done everything, to stand.
—Ephesians 6:12–13 (NIV)

WHY KNOW IT?

✦ Amazon.com lists more than 500 books about spiritual warfare and offers over 20 video games involving demons or demonic powers.[1]

transfuse (trans FYOOZ): to cause to pass from one to another; transmit

You and I are engaged in a war against an invisible enemy. A battle for your choices is waiting for you every day. It's as close as the click of your computer mouse, as alluring as easy money. Yet no matter how enticing the temptation, we are responsible for the decisions we make.

Because of this truth, God has provided a covering, a spiritual armor to defend against the schemes of the devil. This is no ordinary armor, for it was crafted by the Creator Himself. Forget about superheroes you see in movies who count on capes, webs, and technology to perform. The covering that God provides is divinely crafted and divinely bestowed and, therefore, infinite in power.

THINK ABOUT IT:

Think about the power you rely on every day. Is it supernatural or something else?

Get this:

God and Satan *were never* equals.

They *are not* equals.

They *will never be* equals.

Are you ready to *stand* against the enemy? Then let's get to the battle.

*For our struggle is not against flesh and
blood, but against the rulers, against the
authorities, against the powers of this dark
world and against the spiritual forces of evil
in the heavenly realms. Therefore put on the
full armor of God so that when the day of
evil comes, you may be able to stand your
ground, and after you have done everything,
to stand.* —**Ephesians 6:12–13 (NIV)**

The devil is real. You might picture him as a cartoonish
clown—with a tail, red tights, and a pitchfork. That im-
age is fantasy and imagination. The truth is that Satan
is a spiritual being who appears as an angel of light. He
cannot force you to do anything against your will. But he
is wise, and you must also be wise.

No military commander could ever be victorious in
war without a clear understanding and knowledge of his
enemy. Recently, we have seen the U.S. military accom-
plish overwhelming and crushing defeat of conventional
armies in record time. We have learned not to rest on our
victories but to adjust our strategies as knowledge and
understanding of our enemies increases.

Likewise, no Christian could ever be victorious against
the adversary of our soul unless he or she understands
Satan's origin, his method of operation, and his goals.

Why Was Satan Created?
Satan is a fallen angel. Satan was created for the purpose of serving God in heaven, along with the rest of
the angels. The word *angel* comes from the Greek word
angelos (also the root of *Los Angeles*—the city of angels).
Angelos means messenger. So God did not create Satan

to do evil but to be an "angel" or "messenger" of God's glory.

---

infuse (in FYOOZ) : to cause to be permeated with something (as a principle or quality) that alters usually for the better

---

Did God Create Evil? What Went Wrong?

Genesis tells us that when God had finished creating the heavens and the earth and everything in them, "God saw all that He had made, and it was very good" (1:31). Everything that God created was good. God did not create evil, but He did create the *potential* for evil. In other words, rather than forcing all of His creatures to behave in a certain way, God made it possible for some of His creatures to either choose to love and serve Him or choose to rebel against Him.

Humans have this choice, and in a similar way, so did angels. Though the Bible does not give us many of the details, it does tell us that Satan, along with other angels, chose to rebel against God. Of course, none of God's created beings is any match for His power, and He cast these sinful angels out of heaven, sentencing them to punishment in hell (2 Peter 2:4; Jude 6).

> We must not expect a man, unaided from above, should ever be a match for an angel, especially whose intellect has been sharpened by malice.[2]
> —Charles Haddon Spurgeon

Satan knew that God alone is eternal and that God created everything that lives, but he arrogantly rejected God's will, thinking that he knew best. Though Satan and his demons oppose God in the world, trying to tempt us to rebel against our Maker, God is ultimately in control; and His will is "good," "acceptable," and "perfect" (Romans 12:2). When we let sin control our minds and our lives, we demonstrate that we do not really believe that God knows what is best for us or that He loves us and desires the best for our lives. But when you "present your bodies a living sacrifice" and "do not conform to this world, but [are] transformed by the renewing of your mind" (Romans 12:2), then you will be able to recognize just how perfect God's will is and just how harmful the devil's lies are.

All of us struggle with sin on a daily basis. What is ONE THING that you fight daily to control and that hinders you from offering your body as a living sacrifice and being transformed by the renewing of your mind?

_____

_____

_____

Circle ONE that you will work on this week:

pride	ego
anger	selfishness
an unforgiving spirit	lust
friends you have chosen	places you go
what you watch	Internet addictions
wasting time	lack of a quiet time

other _____

What About Demons?
When Satan was cast out of heaven for sinning against God, other rebellious angels were cast out with him

(2 Peter 2:4; Jude 6). While fallen angels are not physical beings, they are real.

Demons are spiteful, wicked beings. Randy Alcorn writes that demons:

+ have an intellect above that of any human;

+ operate within a hierarchy to issue, receive, and carry out orders;

+ wage war against God, righteous angels, and believers;

+ use intelligence gathering, strategy, deploying troops, communicating battle orders, and reporting on the results of engagements as fundamental aspects of warfare;

+ twist, deceive, and mislead people, but they are intimately familiar with the truth they twist.[3]

What Is the Devil's Real Name?

+ This malignant being is referred to throughout the Old and New Testaments as Satan, which comes from a Hebrew word meaning *adversary*.

+ He went from being a beautiful, angelic being to a lowly snake in the grass, referred to as "the serpent" and "the great dragon" (Genesis 3; 2 Corinthians 11:3; Revelation 12:9; 20:2).

+ In the New Testament, he is called the *devil*, a Greek word for accuser, slanderer, deceiver.

+ Jesus refers to him as a murderer and "the father of lies" (John 8:44).

+ Jesus also referred to Satan as "the prince (or ruler) of this world" (John 12:31; 14:30; 16:11) and as "the evil one" (Matthew 13:19).

Though Satan was created to serve God as one of His angels, he rebelled against God and was cast out of God's presence. He became the personification of everything sinful and evil.

Satan's choice immediately knocked him out of his original, uniquely created purpose. Think it through: Are your everyday choices keeping you on track with God's unique purpose for your life?

When faced with temptation, let your decisions honor your Father in heaven, not the father of lies. No Christian should ever desire the lies and temptations of the evil one when God is divine and offers supernatural living in spirit and truth.

Are you easily tempted by the lies of the devil?

Why do you think so many Christian students are so easily misled into believing the lie that life in service to God is not the best life a person can have?

What can you do about it?

_____

_____

_____

Now that you understand *who* Satan is, let us now look at *what* he attempts to do in your life.

_____

_____

_____

diffuse (di FYOOZ) ; to pour out and permit or cause to spread freely; to extend, scatter

As we discussed earlier, success in any battle requires that we *know the enemy*. We must know what he is capable of and what his limitations are.

You know his origin, so now . . .

What Is His Method of Operation?

> *For we do not wrestle against flesh and blood,*
> *but against principalities, against powers,*
> *against the rulers of the darkness of this*
> *age, against spiritual hosts of wickedness in*
> *the heavenly places.* —**Ephesians 6:12**

Before you start blaming your friends for getting you in trouble or get mad at your parents for "ruining your life" (we are such dramatic creatures, aren't we?), remind yourself that your fiercest enemies are not flesh and blood but spiritual powers of wickedness who tempt you to deny God and stop living according to His Word. The battle for our souls is taking place every day.

It is a spiritual battle against *principalities and powers.*

+ They are invisible beings that personify the extremities of evil.

+ They use spiritual weapons, not physical.

+ They present temptations to cheat, steal, and lie.

The Christian leader does not take the spiritual battle lightly. That means we cannot adjust our moral scale to those around us. Instead, we must commit to love and obey Christ and His Word. Only then can we be influential leaders for the glory of God.

What would you like to display to others this week that would set you apart as a leader?

_____

_____

_____

What might keep you from that choice?

_____

_____

_____

Who might keep you from that choice?

_____

_____

_____

What's next, then?

_____

_____

_____

Contrary to popular movie scripts, demons cannot violate our bodies or cause us to levitate. The devil cannot directly interact with us physically, but he does have access to our minds and can influence our choices.

 Don't: Overestimate Satan's power by supposing he can control us against our wills.

Don't: Underestimate Satan's craftiness, an opposite error that is equally wrong and dangerous.

Are you guilty of either or both of these errors?

_____

_____

_____

While "our adversary the devil walks about like a roaring lion, seeking whom he may devour" (1 Peter 5:8), he is a lion on a leash. And the length of his leash is determined by the Lord.

Write one specific thought about a time you overestimated Satan out of fear:

_____

_____

_____

_____

_____

How did that turn out?

Write one specific thought about a time you underestimated Satan because of carelessness:

Have you learned from this mistake, made amends with those you wronged, asked for God's forgiveness and moved on in strength?

If not, make your plans this week to do so. Write it:

When:

Who:

How:

The Bible gives us genuine accounts of Satan's influence over others:

He *deceived* Eve.

✦ "And the Lord God said to the woman, 'What is this you have done?' The woman said, 'The serpent deceived me, and I ate'" (Genesis 3:13).

He *moved* on David and caused him to lose faith in God's will.

✦ "Now Satan stood up against Israel, and moved David to number Israel" (1 Chronicles 21:1).

He *put into the heart of* Judas to sin against Christ.

✦ "And supper being ended, the devil having already put it into the heart of Judas Iscariot, Simon's son, to betray Him" (John 13:2).

He *filled the heart* of Ananias *to lie*.

✦ "But Peter said, 'Ananias, why has Satan filled your heart to lie to the Holy Spirit and keep back part of the price of the land for yourself?'" (Acts 5:3).

He *tempted* Jesus personally.

✦ "And He was there in the wilderness forty days, tempted by Satan, and was with the wild beasts; and the angels ministered to Him" (Mark 1:13).

This adversary *cannot* read our minds. But he *can* influence our thoughts. That is why we must be covered daily with the *full armor* of God. Anything less leaves us wide open to the deceiver. Paul knew this firsthand, and he writes, "Take up the whole armor of God that you may be able to withstand in the evil day, and having done all, to stand" (Ephesians 6:13).

The very force of the words *withstand* and *stand* tell us that we must not and need not be afraid of this enemy of our souls. This covering of armor gives a sure victory, even "in the evil day." Without it, we are exposed to the devil's schemes, and he plays for keeps.

Now that you are beginning to understand the power of the covering God has given you, can you share it with others? Think of one person you know who is struggling in life: how do you think he or she would feel if you explained that there is a great strength available in the Word of God to overcome anger, hatred, bitterness, lust, greed, etc.?

_____

_____

_____

_____

_____

_____

Next week, we will put on the first pieces of the covering—the belt of truth and the breastplate of righteousness. In your Private World this week, ask God to reveal any sin in your life that is keeping you from loving Him and serving Him, from loving others and serving others. He will show you the truth, and the truth will set you free.

Satan's lies and taunts cannot be discerned with the physical ear, but they absolutely do penetrate the mind. We cannot explain how such communication takes place any more than we can explain how our minds can cause the physical synapses of the brain to fire.

[FUSE BOX]

No matter how enticing the temptation,
we are responsible for the final choice.

NOTES

PRIVATE WORLD DEVOTIONS

MONDAY: See it. Read the surrounding passages or chapter for the Key Scripture so that you can get an understanding of the background and context. This helps you to really *see* the verse.

TUESDAY: Hear it. Read the daily Key Scripture and/or surrounding passage out loud, putting your name in, if applicable. For example, <u>John</u> *can do all things through Christ. Thieves have come to destroy* <u>John</u>*, but Jesus has come that* <u>John</u> *might have eternal life.*

WEDNESDAY: Write it. Write the verse and then what it says about:

- ✦ *Others:* Respond, serve, and love as Jesus would.
- ✦ *Me:* Specific attitudes, choices, or habits.
- ✦ *God:* His love, mercy, holiness, peace, joy, etc.

PRIVATE WORLD JOURNAL

I am grateful for—I praise You for—I am feeling—I am thinking—I need help with

PRIVATE WORLD DEVOTIONS *(Continued)*

THURSDAY: Memorize it. Take the verse with you—write it on a card or put it in your phone, iPod, or PDA. Go over it throughout the day so that it begins to *live* in your heart and mind.

FRIDAY: Pray it. Personalize the verse as you pray for yourself or for others or in praise to God. To pray is literally "to think about." Try thinking out loud or writing in your **PRIVATE WORLD JOURNAL.**

SATURDAY: Share it. Ask the Lord to bring someone to mind or in your path today who needs good news. Don't be shy—just let it out! Whether you IM, write, text, tell, or send it, the joy of God's Word will flow from your heart into theirs.

PRAYER REQUESTS

Date	Name	Need	Answer

PRIVATE WORLD JOURNAL

I am grateful for—I praise You for—I am feeling—I am thinking—I need help with

NOTES

CHAPTER 3

THE COVERING OF TRUTH AND RIGHTEOUSNESS

KEY SCRIPTURE

Stand therefore, having girded your waist with truth, having put on the breastplate of righteousness.

—**Ephesians 6:14**

WHY KNOW IT?

✦ Google lists over two million Web sites pertaining to "spiritual warfare" and over twelve thousand sites related to "eRumor" (false information circulated through the Internet).[1]

transfuse (trans FYOOZ): to cause to pass from one to another; transmit

As of this writing, it typically takes 200 milliseconds (thousandths of a second) for a chunk of data to travel from point A anywhere in the world to point B anywhere in the world and back (round trip).[2] In fact, eRumors have become so popular that Web sites like www.truthorfiction.com have popped up in an effort to help distinguish the truth from the tangled web of falsehood.

In an age in which Internet fabrications "travel halfway around the world before truth has had a chance to put its boots on,"[3] the covering of *truth* must be put on with some urgency.

Stand therefore, having girded your waist with truth, having put on the breastplate of righteousness. —**Ephesians 6:14**

infuse (in FYOOZ)'. to cause to be permeated with something (as a principle or quality) that alters usually for the better

The Belt of Truth

In his book *Time for Truth,* Os Guinness explains, "The Christian faith is not true because it works; it works because it is true. It is not true because we experience it; we experience it—deeply and gloriously—because it is true. It is not simply 'true for us'; it is true for any who seek in order to find, because truth is true even if nobody believes it, and falsehood is false even if everybody believes it. That is why truth does not yield to opinion, fashion, numbers, office, or sincerity—it is simply true and that is the end of it."[4]

Which one has had more influence over you this year so far?

✦ The opinion of the crowd

✦ The truth of God's Word

What is the ONE spiritual truth that has made the greatest impact on your life this year?

_____

_____

_____

_____

"Stand therefore . . . "

As your waist is the center of your body, so the belt of truth is central to the full armor of God.

Paul reminds the believer again to *stand*—that is, to maintain his ground, not giving in to opinion or pressure but always to what is true.

This *stand* is not a passive one, for the believer has put on or *girded* himself with the belt of truth. The soldier was to *gird his loins* at all times so that he could be ready at a moment's notice for action. A robe that was not girded indicated a soldier who was not ready to fight.

TRUTH

1a: FIDELITY CONSTANCY

b: sincerity in action, character, and utterance.

2a(1): the state of being the case: FACT

(2): the body of real things, events, and facts: ACTUALITY

(3): *often capitalized:* a transcendent fundamental or spiritual reality

b: a judgment, proposition, or idea that is true or accepted as true ‹*truths* of thermodynamics›

c: the body of true statements and propositions.[5]

" . . . having girded your waist with truth . . . "

What is this *truth* that we are to bind ourselves with?

- ◆ *Truth* is an aspect of the nature of God Himself. "He is the Rock, His work is perfect; for all His ways are justice, a God of truth and without injustice; righteous and upright is He" (Deuteronomy 32:4).

- ◆ To put on the *belt of truth* is to put on Christ. "Jesus said to him, 'I am the way, the truth, and the life. No one comes to the Father except through Me'" (John 14:6).

NOTE: This attribute of God is in direct contrast to Satan, who is called "the father of lies" (John 8:44).

Truth is essential to a realistic worldview.

- ◆ Without truth, our view of reality becomes seriously skewed and we rely more on rumor and opinion than the Word of God.

How do we discern truth? Everyone seems to have his or her own version of truth, and each person claims his or her belief as the "true" one.

For a statement or belief to be true, it must:

- ◆ correspond to reality (the way things really are in the world);

- ◆ be internally consistent (it doesn't contradict itself);

- ◆ be livable (it can be consistently lived out).

diffuse (di FYOOZ): to pour out and permit or cause to spread freely; to extend, scatter

The Breastplate of Righteousness

What you believe affects the way you behave and ultimately who you become. The apostle Paul knew this, and he carefully joined *truth* in words with *righteousness* in works.

✦ To believe in truth is to live out moral virtue.

✦ Truth without righteousness is repulsive.

✦ A worldview that is not joined to righteousness has no moral authority to share.

" . . . having put on the breastplate of righteousness."

The *breastplate* was similar to a modern-day bulletproof vest. As a breastplate or bulletproof vest is a physical heart protector, so the breastplate of righteousness is a spiritual heart protector.

Fighting in Paul's day was conducted up close and personal, so the quickest way to slay the enemy was to go directly for a stab in the heart. It would have been foolish for a Roman soldier to engage a physical enemy without a breastplate.

To face the enemy of our souls without the covering of the *breastplate of righteousness* is just as foolish and carries more hazardous consequences.

Without it, we are not only weak, but we leave ourselves helpless in the invisible spiritual war.

RIGHTEOUSNESS

1: acting in accord with divine or moral law: free from guilt or sin

2a: morally right or justifiable ⟨a *righteous* decision⟩

b: arising from an outraged sense of justice or morality ⟨*righteous* indignation⟩

3: *slang:* GENUINE, GOOD.[6]

Think about a time when you have felt pressure to bend your Christian beliefs by others who use excuses like, "Everyone does it." "It's not as bad as so-and-so." "It's different today." Weigh such opinions or "truths" against the standard of righteousness exemplified by Jesus Christ. Do they measure up? If not, throw them out!

Before examining what true righteousness is, we must understand how it can be attained.

We do not become righteous through anything we can do. The only righteous one is God Himself, and we receive the righteousness of God the Son, Jesus Christ, when we accept His perfect life and His death on our behalf and submit to Him as Lord of our lives. Imagine the teacher of your most difficult class announcing that everyone had failed the final exam, but everyone would not only pass but receive an A + because he had decided to take the test himself and credit his grade to everyone in the class. God's crediting of Christ's righteousness to us is like this, but so much greater. Righteousness isn't just about passing a class; it determines our eternal destiny! What a gift!

So what is righteousness?

Righteousness is:

- the core of Christianity compressed into a single word;
- the actual doing and completing the will of God;
- a right relation with Him;
- obedience through love;
- the result of salvation through faith;
- spiritual discipline of the whole person: body and soul;

✦ accountability of our actions, words, and thoughts.

Righteousness is **not**:

✦ our own good works;

✦ attained through deliverance from demons;

✦ an act of pride;

✦ selective sinfulness;

✦ hypocritical judgmentalism.

In John 8:2–11, the self-righteous Pharisees brought an adulterous woman to Jesus. They acted as though their intentions were good, but they were not. Jesus saw through their pretension and gave no honor to their proclamation of self-righteousness. He shrewdly shamed the Pharisees for their hypocrisy and then demonstrated God's forgiveness for the woman and called her to repentance.

 What do I do when others bring rumors and judgmental accusations to me?

_____

_____

_____

GROUP DISCUSSION

Have you ever had someone bring you a "prayer request" that was actually a disguise for gossip?

_____

_____

_____

How should we handle this?

- ✦ Decide today not to ever repeat a rumor. Nothing good can come from repeating it.

- ✦ Decide today to love others regardless of what is said about them. Refuse to listen to gossip and stand ready to forgive those who sin against you. In so doing, you will reflect the love of Christ.

Those who wish to emulate Tiger Woods do not become Tigerlike by simply donning a Nike swoosh, nor do they win the Grand Slam of golf by merely repeating Nike's "Just do it" slogan. Instead, they become Tigerlike through mental and physical discipline.

Similarly, those who wish to emulate Jesus Christ do not become Christlike by simply taking on the appearance of Christianity, nor do they win the good fight by merely mouthing Christian slogans. Instead, they become Christlike by offering themselves to God as "a living sacrifice" (Romans 12:1).

Prayer, fasting, and sacrifice characterized the life of Christ. In like fashion, such spiritual disciplines must characterize the lives of those who sincerely desire to become Christlike.

What can you begin to do this week to become more Christlike?

_____

_____

_____

Your Private World this week:

In prayer: Commit to spending at least five minutes each day praying through praise psalms.

When can you do this?

In fasting: Choose to eliminate one meal from one day and put that money in a missions fund.

Which meal?

In sacrifice: Ask God to help you resist the temptation of a particular sinful behavior or attitude that you struggle with.

Which behavior or attitude?

[FUSE BOX]

Truth and righteousness cannot be separated. They are a strong covering for your heart and life.

PRIVATE WORLD DEVOTIONS

MONDAY: See it. Read the surrounding passages or chapter for the Key Scripture so that you can get an understanding of the background and context. This helps you to really *see* the verse.

TUESDAY: Hear it. Read the daily Key Scripture and/or surrounding passage out loud, putting your name in, if applicable. For example, <u>John</u> *can do all things through Christ. Thieves have come to destroy* <u>John</u>, *but Jesus has come that* <u>John</u> *might have eternal life.*

WEDNESDAY: Write it. Write the verse and then what it says about:

✦ *Others:* Respond, serve, and love as Jesus would.

✦ *Me:* Specific attitudes, choices, or habits.

✦ *God:* His love, mercy, holiness, peace, joy, etc.

PRIVATE WORLD JOURNAL

I am grateful for—I praise You for—I am feeling—I am thinking—I need help with

PRIVATE WORLD DEVOTIONS *(Continued)*

THURSDAY: Memorize it. Take the verse with you—write it on a card or put it in your phone, iPod, or PDA. Go over it throughout the day so that it begins to *live* in your heart and mind.

FRIDAY: Pray it. Personalize the verse as you pray for yourself or for others or in praise to God. To pray is literally "to think about." Try thinking out loud or writing in your **PRIVATE WORLD JOURNAL.**

SATURDAY: Share it. Ask the Lord to bring someone to mind or in your path today who needs good news. Don't be shy—just let it out! Whether you IM, write, text, tell, or send it, the joy of God's Word will flow from your heart into theirs.

PRAYER REQUESTS

Date	Name	Need	Answer

PRIVATE WORLD JOURNAL

*I am grateful for—I praise You for—I am
feeling—I am thinking—I need help with*

NOTES

CHAPTER 4

THE COVERING OF PEACE

KEY SCRIPTURE

Stand . . . having shod your feet with the preparation of the gospel of peace.

—Ephesians 6:14–15

WHY KNOW IT?

✦ One out of every eight born again people (13%) made their profession of faith while 18 to 21 years old.[1]

✦ Forty-nine percent of born again Christians shared their faith in Christ in the past year by taking a non-Christian friend to church so they could hear the gospel.[2]

transfuse (trans FYOOZ)` ; to cause to pass from one to another; transmit

Have you ever shied away from sharing the gospel with people because you were afraid you might not be able to answer their questions? Are you confident enough in your understanding of the gospel to take every opportunity to share it with others? Perhaps the most common reason students give for failing to share the gospel is that they are afraid they will not know what to say.

While we all must be ready to share the gospel whenever we have opportunity, it is important to remember that we are responsible for the process of evangelism, not for the results.

What about you? Do you know what to say when someone asks you about your faith? Has your prayer, meditation, and study time in your Private World prepared you to confidently proclaim and defend the gospel of peace?

Stand . . . having shod your feet
with the preparation of the gospel of
peace. —**Ephesians 6:14–15**

The Lord has a tailor-made, custom-fitted covering available for you. The need for such is seen in the urgent warnings of Scripture concerning spiritual warfare.

infuse (in FYOOZ)¦ to cause to be permeated with something (as a principle or quality) that alters usually for the better

" . . . having shod your feet . . . "

Having centered ourselves with truth and guarded our heart with righteousness, we now move to the feet. The *feet* are discussed in this verse to tell us that this gospel of peace:

✦ goes with us daily as we walk through life;

✦ is available through every difficulty, discouragement, illness, and trial;

✦ acts as a protection by preparing us to engage in spiritual warfare.

Why does the covering speak of *feet?* These seem unimportant when related to guarding the heart. Yet think about Shaquille O'Neal, the famous NBA player who stands 7'1" tall and wears size 22 shoes. This colossal man is an outright star when it comes to basketball. But on more than one occasion, this 300-pound giant has been sidelined because of one toe! Much as he hates to admit it, when his toes ache, Shaq doesn't have the same quickness to the ball and can't block as many shots. To prepare him for success, he is fitted with a special pair of sneakers. No expense is spared.

As Shaq's sneakers are essential to winning basketball wars, so, too, our feet must be properly fitted in order to prevail in spiritual warfare. All the skills and resources humanity has to offer have been brought to bear on protecting the feet of a $30-million-per-year basketball star. That, however, pales by comparison to the price that was paid to have our "feet shod with the preparation of the gospel of peace."

" . . . with the preparation . . . "

What shoes are to our feet, spiritual readiness is to our souls.

The shoes of the ancient soldier were leather sandals, a protection that allowed them to cover a variety of terrains. Likewise, the gospel of peace allows us to be in a constant state of *preparation* or readiness for battle.

The word *prepared* is a revealing term. It comes from the Latin *paro*, which has several meanings:

◆ *to be pointed in the right direction.* The right direction is twofold: to live each day in moral excellence and obedience to Jesus Christ, who says, "I am the way" (John 14:6); and to seek God's perfect will for your life.

◆ *to be made complete.* We are complete when we have received Christ as our Savior. Don't make the mistake of knowing *about* Christ, but not *knowing Christ personally.*

✦ *to be equipped for battle.* We are only equipped for battle when we put on the covering provided by the Lord against spiritual warfare as outlined in Ephesians 6. Just as the soldier's body must be protected in physical warfare, so must our hearts and minds be protected for us to triumph in spiritual warfare. By focusing on and proclaiming the gospel of peace, we are reminded of whose side in this battle we are on—the side that has already triumphed through Jesus's death on the cross and resurrection from the dead.

Think about how you prepare for a day at school. Do you run out the door, or can you describe yourself as prepared using the definition above?

_____

_____

_____

_____

Now think about how you prepare to explain the gospel to your friends and family members. Do you neglect to study God's Word and then simply hope that you will have answers to their questions when they ask, or do you diligently study God's Word, meditating on it and examining the reasons for your faith so that you can "always be ready to give a defense to everyone who asks you a reason for the hope that is in you" (1 Peter 3:15)?

_____

_____

_____

_____

Let's think about a change:

✦ *to be pointed in the right direction.*

You need to know the sure truth as taught in Scripture, and you need to be right with God and filled with His Spirit.

✦ Are you ready to make the right choice today when temptation hits?

✦ Do you understand the meaning of the gospel of peace?

✦ Do you recognize the importance of sharing this gospel?

> We are not responsible for the results of evangelism, only for the process.

✦ *to be made complete.*

Have you come to the place in your spiritual life where you no longer have a "borrowed faith" from your friends or parents but a personal relationship with Christ?

✦ *to be equipped for battle.*

Have you *put on* truth and righteousness before you walk out the door?

Are you ready to defend the truth of God's Word and live in a way that is pleasing to Him?

Are you prepared to take every opportunity to share the gospel of peace?

What is ONE THING out of the preceding list that you can change this week?

_____

_____

_____

How will you do this?

_____

_____

_____

Who can you ask for help?

_____

_____

_____

What part does your Private World play in this?

_____

_____

_____

" . . . *of the gospel of peace.*"
The word *gospel* means God's spell—the Word of God— or, according to others, "good spell" or good news. It

is the rendering of the Greek *evangelion,* meaning good message.[3] It is literally *good news!* And the good news is this—that we can have peace with God!

As Paul wrote to the Romans, "Therefore, having been justified by faith, we have peace with God through our Lord Jesus Christ" (Romans 5:1). We were once enemies of God, living in rebellion against Him, but because Christ died for us, paid the price for our sin, rose victorious over death, and ever lives to love us, our relationship with God has been restored and we live in peace with the holy Creator of the universe.

Here, peace is not simply feeling calm or relaxed. Instead, this peace is contrasted with brokenness in relationship. It is often very difficult for us to forgive those who have wronged us, but when we do, we restore a broken relationship and can continue to live in peace with each other.

Our sinful rebellion against God resulted in a broken relationship with Him. And as the righteous Judge of the universe, God could not allow that relationship to be restored without a just punishment for our sin.

Because He knew that we would never be able to pay for our own sins and because of His great love for us, God gave His only Son as the sacrifice for our sin. That is extremely good news! We no longer need to fear the punishment of God for our sins, but instead can live in peace with Him.

> Thou hast made us for thyself, O Lord, and our hearts are restless until they find their rest in thee.
> —St. Augustine

Do you have peace with God?

_____

_____

_____

Understanding this gospel of peace can also lead to another kind of peace in our lives—the kind of peace that is contrasted with worry, anxiety, and guilt. When we understand the incredible magnitude of this gift of God and the intensity of His love for us, then we have peace regardless of our circumstances or culture.

Charles Spurgeon, England's most famous pastor in the late nineteenth century, wrote: "We believe in a gospel that was formed in the purpose of God from all eternity,

> designed with infinite wisdom;
>
> wrought out at an enormous expense, costing nothing less than the blood of Jesus;
>
> brought home by the infinite power of the Holy Spirit;
>
> a gospel full of blessings, and one of which would outweigh a world in price;
>
> a gospel as free as it is full;
>
> a gospel everlasting and immutable;
>
> a gospel of which we can never think too much, whose praises we can never exaggerate!"[4]

Most Christian teens have heard the gospel since they were just small children. In your life, it may now feel "routine" to hear it.

Select one phrase from the preceding quote that is meaningful to you. Write it here:

_____

_____

_____

Now take a moment to thank the Lord for this gospel of peace with Him and what it means for your life.

Spend some time this week with Charles Spurgeon's quote, taking it apart piece by piece. Journal your thoughts as you do so, offering thanks to God for His great salvation.

Peace with God

> *Therefore, having been justified by faith,*
> *we have peace with God through our*
> *Lord Jesus Christ.* —**Romans 5:1**

The *gospel of peace* is so named because it provides us *peace with God.* How can you, a sinner, have peace with a holy God? Because the holy God so loved you that He gave His only Son as an atoning sacrifice for sin on your behalf. You must understand that no matter what you have done, thought, or said, your heavenly Father stands ready to forgive you today on account of Christ.

Peace with God is not a funeral term. It is not for the dying. It is for the living, every day, for everyone. Through salvation by faith in Christ, we have:

+ *an intimate relationship with God.* "But now in Christ Jesus you who once were far off have been brought near by the blood of Christ" (Ephesians 2:13).

+ *been made His child.* "But as many as received Him, to them He gave the right to become children of God, to those who believe in His name" (John 1:12).

+ *received mercy instead of the just punishment for our sins.* "Who once were not a people but are now the people of God, who had not obtained mercy but now have obtained mercy" (1 Peter 2:10).

Sometimes we allow our sins to keep us separated from God. Whether because we are prideful, embarrassed, or ashamed, instead of turning back *to* Him in repentance, we stubbornly try to stay *away* from Him. To do so is to reject His love and His offer of forgiveness.

Is there anything you need to ask His forgiveness for in your life? Confess to Him now, and know that He has surely forgiven you.

We have peace with God because *He loved us first.* He does not hold a grudge. He forgives completely, and by accepting this forgiveness we receive eternal life and peace with God.

diffuse (di FYOOZ) : to pour out and permit or cause to spread freely; to extend, scatter

Peace with Others

> When a man's ways please the Lord,
> He makes even his enemies to be at
> peace with him. —**Proverbs 16:7**

While we cannot make anyone love us, we can love everyone. Fitted with the gospel of peace, we can tread confidently through conflict and controversy with other Christians. Put another way, submission to God and a life beyond reproach will disarm your adversaries.

As Peter promises, addressing the world with a clear conscience will cause "those who revile your good conduct in Christ" to be "ashamed" (1 Peter 3:16).

Now for teens, this is a big deal. During these years, tempers easily flare, feelings are easily hurt, and hearts are broken.

✦ Only 3% of teens say they never get angry.

✦ The most popular response to anger among teens is to walk away from or ignore it.

✦ Only 4% of teens confront or discuss their anger with the person who angered them.[5]

What are some things that teens get angry with each other about? List five:

Are any of these worth ruining a relationship over?

GROUP DISCUSSION

Discuss Spurgeon's previous quote about "an unwilling-ness to think badly of any Christian." Is that possible?

_____

_____

_____

How do you think adopting that action would change your youth group?

_____

_____

_____

Peace in the Midst of Stress or Discouragement

> _And the peace of God, which surpasses_
> _all understanding, will guard your hearts_
> _and minds through Christ Jesus._
> **—Philippians 4:7**

God does not promise us a magic solution to every problem, but He does promise us peace in the midst of life's storms. With God's peace, we can stand firm in distress, disease, destruction, and even death. For when our burden of sin has been removed, all other burdens become bearable.

Amy Allen wrote of her mom's courageous faith and the resulting peace in her journal, and she shares it with you today:

When my mom was experiencing chemotherapy treatments every week, she was so sick. She already lost her hair and was weak beyond belief. She asked my dad not to go with her to her treatments so that she could help encourage other women in the chemo room. Her strong conviction that she was to share Jesus with these other cancer patients, and her desire to encourage these women was an inspiration to me. When she passed away and walked into heaven, there were eight former cancer patients my mom led to Jesus who met her on streets of gold and welcomed her to heaven.

The *gospel of peace* is a preview of the promise of perfect peace in paradise. As a student, stress and conflict confront you daily, but believers who stand firm with their feet fitted with the gospel of peace are only a step away from peace and confidence.

Throughout the day, think about the great gift of peace with God. This peace is a strong defense against the depression and discouragement that can come from the daily stress of life.

Either this great gospel is true, or it isn't! Either we can trust God or we can't! You must choose today.

FUSE BOX

When we accept God's gift of peace with the Creator and Lover of our souls, we are spiritually ready to face all the trials and tribulations life brings our way.

PRIVATE WORLD DEVOTIONS

MONDAY: See it. Read the surrounding passages or chapter for the Key Scripture so that you can get an understanding of the background and context. This helps you to really *see* the verse.

TUESDAY: Hear it. Read the daily Key Scripture and/or surrounding passage out loud, putting your name in, if applicable. For example, <u>John</u> *can do all things through Christ. Thieves have come to destroy* <u>John</u>, *but Jesus has come that* <u>John</u> *might have eternal life.*

WEDNESDAY: Write it. Write the verse and then what it says about:

✦ *Others:* Respond, serve, and love as Jesus would.

✦ *Me:* Specific attitudes, choices, or habits.

✦ *God:* His love, mercy, holiness, peace, joy, etc.

PRIVATE WORLD JOURNAL

I am grateful for—I praise You for—I am feeling—I am thinking—I need help with

PRIVATE WORLD DEVOTIONS *(Continued)*

THURSDAY: Memorize it. Take the verse with you—write it on a card or put it in your phone, iPod, or PDA. Go over it throughout the day so that it begins to *live* in your heart and mind.

FRIDAY: Pray it. Personalize the verse as you pray for yourself or for others or in praise to God. To pray is literally "to think about." Try thinking out loud or writing in your **PRIVATE WORLD JOURNAL.**

SATURDAY: Share it. Ask the Lord to bring someone to mind or in your path today who needs good news. Don't be shy—just let it out! Whether you IM, write, text, tell, or send it, the joy of God's Word will flow from your heart into theirs.

PRAYER REQUESTS

Date	Name	Need	Answer

PRIVATE WORLD JOURNAL

I am grateful for—I praise You for—I am feeling—I am thinking—I need help with

NOTES

CHAPTER 5

THE COVERING OF FAITH

KEY SCRIPTURE

Above all, taking the shield of faith with which you will be able to quench all the fiery darts of the wicked one.
—**Ephesians 6:16**

WHY KNOW IT?

✦ 56% of teens feel that their religious faith is very important in their life.[1]

✦ Adolescents who perceive faith as important in their lives are less likely to smoke cigarettes, drink alcohol, or use drugs.[2]

transfuse (trans FYOOZ)'; to cause to pass from one to another; transmit

Long before extreme sports, there was extreme faith. If you doubt this, read Hebrews 11. From the beginning of human history, Satan set out to establish a cosmic war between God's goodness and his own evil.

✦ In every recorded victory, faith was the captain.

✦ In every recorded defeat, a doubtful heart gave into evil actions.

Scripture is full of stories of men and women who were able to persevere through incredibly trying circumstances because of their profound faith in God. Job, one of God's champions, gives us a true narrative that could be called the "Book of Extreme Faith." Within its pages is the story of Job's ultimate test against a direct and personal attack by Satan and his sure victory through faith.

Above all, taking the shield of faith with which you will be able to quench all the fiery darts of the wicked one. **—Ephesians 6:16**

"And the LORD said to Satan, 'From where do you come?' So Satan answered the LORD and said, 'From going to and fro on the earth, and from walking back and forth on it.' Then the LORD said to Satan, 'Have you considered My servant Job, that there is none like him on the earth, a blameless and upright man, one who fears God and shuns evil?' So Satan answered the LORD and said, 'Does Job fear God for nothing? Have You not made a hedge around him, around his household, and around all that he has on every side? You have blessed the work of his hands, and his possessions have increased in the land. But now, stretch out Your hand and touch all that he has, and he will surely curse You to Your face!' And the LORD said to Satan, 'Behold, all that he has is in your power; only do not lay a hand on his person.' So Satan went out from the presence of the LORD" (Job 1:7–12).

✦ Satan thought this test out.

He looked at Job's strengths and at his possible weaknesses.

He planned with precision.

✦ God stood on the side of his beloved Job.

He allowed the test,
but He also set the limitations.

infuse (in FYOOZ) : to cause to be permeated with something (as a principle or quality) that alters usually for the better

Job endured more tragedy in a single day than most people experience in an entire lifetime.

In the span of a few hours:

✦ Job's servants were slaughtered;

✦ His oxen, donkeys, and camels were stolen in two separate raids;

✦ His sheep were killed by fire;

✦ His seven sons and three daughters perished in a collapsing house.

THINK ABOUT IT:

How would you respond to this devastation and crisis?

_____

_____

_____

_____

Job's great response is a declaration of faith in God. "He said: 'Naked I came from my mother's womb, and naked shall I return there. The LORD gave, and the LORD has taken away; blessed be the name of the LORD.' In all this Job did not sin nor charge God with wrong" (Job 1:21–22).

Definition of Faith

Faith is:

+ not simply knowledge or assent, but a channel of living trust;

+ not blind or simpleminded, but based on reason and evidence;

+ not a crutch, but the only reasonable response to God, who has shown Himself to be faithful;

+ relying on God alone to save us from sin and death;

+ believing that God wants the best for our lives and that He is always in control, regardless of circumstances;

+ knowing that God has given all that we have and will continue to give all that we need;

+ praising God in the midst of suffering, because we know that He is faithful.

What ONE THING do you want to choose to believe with confidence this week? Write it by putting your name in the sentence.

Faith is:

_____

_____

_____

_____

Satan could not believe that Job would not curse God. Possibly, this made him angry, and he changed his plan to an even more evil and direct hit.

"Then the LORD said to Satan, 'Have you considered My servant Job, that there is none like him on the earth, a blameless and upright man, one who fears God and shuns evil? And still he holds fast to his integrity, although you incited Me against him, to destroy him without cause.' So Satan answered the LORD and said, 'Skin for skin! Yes, all that a man has he will give for his life. But stretch out Your hand now, and touch his bone and his flesh, and he will surely curse You to Your face!' And the LORD said to Satan, 'Behold, he is in your hand, but spare his life'" (Job 2:3–6).

Declaration of the Will

Once again, God allowed the test, but He set the limitations:

- ✦ Job's body was covered with boils.

- ✦ His wife cursed God and turned against him.

- ✦ His friends began to blame Job for his troubles.

Through it all, Job stood fast in his genuine, personal faith. "'Shall we indeed accept good from God, and shall we not accept adversity?' In all this Job did not sin with his lips" (Job 2:10).

✦ Faith often begins with a declaration of the will.

✦ Faith grows through a guarded heart.

✦ Faith depends on the faithfulness of God.

In this cosmic contest between Satan and God, Job became the subject of an extreme test of faith.

✦ God affirmed Job's faith as firm and faultless.

✦ Satan assailed Job's faith as fickle and fleeting.

Job's faith endured, and his eternal perspective on faith is forever enshrined in the words, "Though He slay me, yet will I trust Him" (Job 13:15).

Consider some of the difficulties you experienced this year:

✦ family

✦ friends

✦ school

✦ disappointments

✦ betrayal

✦ health

✦ finances

What were your first thoughts, your first words in the situation?

Using the definitions of *faith* above, take a current difficulty in your life and put it through the FAITH test by praying through these steps:

✦ *Faith begins with a declaration of the will.*

In the midst of this difficulty, I, _____, declare faith in God.

✦ *Faith grows through a guarded heart.*

In the midst of this difficulty, I, _____, will guard my heart against complaining, negative thoughts, ingratitude, and selfishness.

✦ *Faith depends on the faithfulness of God.*

I will continue to believe that God is powerful to work His will in and through my life.

Faith Is the Shield That Covers All Parts of the Armor

Above all, taking the shield of faith with which you will be able to quench all the fiery darts of the wicked one. —**Ephesians 6:16**

Job's declaration of faith was no accident; it was not a random thought. With the shield of faith in hand, Job was enabled to stand strong and steadfast against persecutions, temptations, and even the blasphemous thoughts Satan whispered in his ear.

Satan was able to scorch Job's shield, but he was unable to sear his soul.

To the covering of *truth, righteousness,* and *peace,* we must now add "the shield of faith with which you will be able to quench all the fiery darts of the wicked one."

Once again, God has made provision for victory. As the ancient shield covered the body, so faith covers our entire being:

✦ When Satan attacks our heads, the hand of faith holds fast to the truth that God loves us and He is in control.

✦ When Satan attacks our hearts, the hand of faith holds fast to truth and acts of righteousness, or right living.

Paul introduces the shield of faith "above all," because it is the shield of faith that covers all other pieces of the armor. It is the shield of faith that is able to move to any part of our being or body that is being attacked.

Every other piece of the full armor of God must inevitably operate in conjunction with faith. In ancient warfare, "the shield was prized by a soldier above all other pieces of armor. He counted it a greater shame to lose his shield than to lose the battle, and therefore he would not part with it even when he was under the very foot of the enemy, but esteemed it an honor to die with his shield in his hand."[3]

Faith Is the Only Way to Please God

> But without faith it is impossible to please Him, for he who comes to God must believe that He is, and that He is a rewarder of those who diligently seek Him. —**Hebrews 11:6**

Faith . . .

✦ is ultimately rooted and grounded in the nature of God Himself;

✦ believes that God means to reward our faithfulness;

✦ is a channel of living trust—an assurance—that stretches from man to God.

Nothing is more crucial to faith than a proper understanding of who and what Satan's limitations are:

GOD	SATAN
Truth	Father of lies
Faithful and true	Deceiver
Creator	Destroyer
Perfect in wisdom	Evil schemer
Omnipotent (all-powerful)	Limited by God in his power
Supreme authority	Will one day be banished for eternity
Omniscient (all-knowing)	Cannot see the future or read thoughts
Omnipresent (everywhere)	Can only be in one place at one time

Look at the chart above of God's attributes. Decide today to select one each day and spend time in prayer of gratitude for that attribute. As these become familiar to your heart, they will spring to your mind in times of difficulty.

GROUP DISCUSSION

What is the first attribute of God that comes to mind as a powerful feeder of your personal faith?

_____

_____

_____

Faith Is Evidence of What Cannot Be Seen

This has well been called the age of information. We can access any information or answer to any question on the Internet in a nanosecond. There seems to be no limit to the amount of information available to us.

But our knowledge of the world is limited—only God is omniscient. Sometimes our experiences are hard to understand, and it is hard to trust in God's promise of salvation. Yet He has demonstrated through the death and resurrection of His Son that He is powerful to overcome all evil, even death, and that He truly loves us; so we can know that He will do as He has promised.

Indeed, the greatest demonstration of faith is trusting God even when we do not understand. "Now faith is the substance of things hoped for, the evidence of things not seen" (Hebrews 11:1).

This the confidence demonstrated by Job as "still he holds fast to his integrity" (Job 2:3). He trusted God in spite the whirlwind that threatened to blow his life into oblivion.

Faith Must Be Demonstrated to Be Genuine

Paul demonstrated this same die-hard faith. "In labors more abundant, in stripes above measure, in prisons more frequently, in deaths often. From the Jews five times I received forty stripes minus one. Three times I was beaten with rods; once I was stoned; three times I was shipwrecked; a night and a day I have been in the deep; in journeys often, in perils of waters, in perils of robbers, in perils of my own countrymen, in perils of the Gentiles, in perils in the city, in perils in the wilderness, in perils in the sea, in perils among false brethren; in weariness and toil, in sleeplessness often, in hunger and thirst, in fasting often, in cold and nakedness" (2 Corinthians 11:23–27).

Paul's faith, like that of Job, was not fixed on his temporary circumstances, but on God's personal, intense, abiding love.

In Romans 8:37–39, Paul writes, "Yet in all these things we are more than conquerors through Him who loved us. For I am persuaded that neither death nor life, nor angels nor principalities nor powers, nor things present nor things to come, nor height nor depth, nor any other created thing, shall be able to separate us from the love of God which is in Christ Jesus our Lord."

diffuse (di FYOOZ); to pour out and permit or cause to spread freely; to extend, scatter

The faith that serves to protect us in spiritual warfare is not to be confused with mere knowledge.

One out of every six adults in America has heard Billy Graham preach in person, and 85 percent of the adults in America have watched him on television.[4] But one in six adults has not professed faith in Christ; 85 percent of adults do not claim to have a personal salvation. The point?

Knowledge Is Not the Same As Saving Faith

True disciples of Christ, however, have what Scripture describes as genuine justifying faith—a faith that not only knows about the gospel and agrees that its content is fact but lives out a faith by which they are transformed.

 How do you describe saving faith?

When you sat down in a chair, did you ask yourself if the chair would be able to hold you up? No, you had the faith to sit it in without question. If you get up from that chair and transfer your body to another chair, then you, in actuality, transfer your "trust" to that chair as well.

Saving faith is when we transfer our trust from our own ability to be "good enough" to get to heaven to the gift of grace through faith in Christ's death on the cross. True salvation is only found in genuine faith in what Christ has already done, not in what we try to do.

This "chair" exercise, when played out, is a great way to understand a transfer of trust. Pray that the Lord will give you the opportunity to share it with someone this week.

The Covering of Faith Strengthens Us to Live for Christ with Confidence

Faith focuses on:

+ eternity rather than temporary pleasure;

+ life from God's point of view;

+ victory instead of defeat.

Genuine Saving Faith Acts As a Testimony to the Generations Yet to Come

Some have asked the question, "How could God have allowed this? Didn't He love Job?" Read the passage again: "Then the LORD said to Satan, 'Have you considered My servant Job, that there is none like him on the earth, a blameless and upright man, one who fears God and shuns evil?' So Satan answered the LORD and said, 'Does Job fear God for nothing?'" (Job 1:8–9).

Think about this: Job was not just *allowed* to suffer; he was *chosen* to suffer. Why? Remember that God knows our thoughts and our future—what we think now and what we will do as a result of those thoughts.

Satan asked God, "Does Your child, Job, love You only because of all the good You give him?" Remember that this enemy does not understand love.

Satan was an angel of God who witnessed firsthand God's glory. Yet Satan *did not love God!* In this passage, Satan cannot believe that *man* could love God when Satan and his angels did not. God said, "Watch and see what true faith and love are."

> For whatever is born of God overcomes the world. And this is the victory that has overcome the world—our faith.
>
> —1 John 5:4

Since you might not have time to read the whole book of Job, let's skip to the end and see how it turned out: "And the LORD restored Job's losses when he prayed for his friends. Indeed the LORD gave Job twice as much as he had before" (Job 42:10).

Satan hates it when we pass the test. He does not want the world to know that love can be genuine, that faith can be powerful.

Decide today: *I will* let the world know . . .

FUSE BOX

Faith understands that God works together every moment of our lives, every circumstance, to bring about His good, pleasing, and perfect purpose for our lives.

PRIVATE WORLD DEVOTIONS

MONDAY: See it. Read the surrounding passages or chapter for the Key Scripture so that you can get an understanding of the background and context. This helps you to really *see* the verse.

TUESDAY: Hear it. Read the daily Key Scripture and/or surrounding passage out loud, putting your name in, if applicable. For example, <u>John</u> *can do all things through Christ. Thieves have come to destroy* <u>John</u>*, but Jesus has come that* <u>John</u> *might have eternal life.*

WEDNESDAY: Write it. Write the verse and then what it says about:

+ *Others:* Respond, serve, and love as Jesus would.
+ *Me:* Specific attitudes, choices, or habits.
+ *God:* His love, mercy, holiness, peace, joy, etc.

PRIVATE WORLD JOURNAL

*I am grateful for—I praise You for—I am
feeling—I am thinking—I need help with*

PRIVATE WORLD DEVOTIONS *(Continued)*

THURSDAY: Memorize it. Take the verse with you—write it on a card or put it in your phone, iPod, or PDA. Go over it throughout the day so that it begins to *live* in your heart and mind.

FRIDAY: Pray it. Personalize the verse as you pray for yourself or for others or in praise to God. To pray is literally "to think about." Try thinking out loud or writing in your **PRIVATE WORLD JOURNAL.**

SATURDAY: Share it. Ask the Lord to bring someone to mind or in your path today who needs good news. Don't be shy—just let it out! Whether you IM, write, text, tell, or send it, the joy of God's Word will flow from your heart into theirs.

PRAYER REQUESTS

Date	Name	Need	Answer

PRIVATE WORLD JOURNAL

I am grateful for—I praise You for—I am feeling—I am thinking—I need help with

NOTES

CHAPTER 6

THE COVERING OF SALVATION

KEY SCRIPTURE

And take the helmet of salvation . . .
—**Ephesians 6:17**

WHY KNOW IT?

✦ Teens list death as #3 on their top ten list of fears.[1]

✦ Most Americans believe in life after death.[2]

transfuse (trans FYOOZ): to cause to pass from one to another; transmit

There are as many opinions about the definition of eternal life as there are colors: reincarnation, an actual heaven, a "presence" with God, reunion with family and friends, a state of mind, and so on.

There are equally as many opinions about what you must do to attain eternal life: through religion, by being baptized, by being "good," through good works, or even "just because." Some even dare to go so far as to say, "Because I'm not as bad as other people."

These are *opinions*, but *not truth*.

And take the helmet of salvation . . .
—Ephesians 6:17

Throughout the last few lessons, we have been talking about the covering that keeps the heart from sin and error—the covering of truth, righteousness, peace, and faith. The covering of salvation is different from the previous pieces of armor in two important ways:

1. The defense switches from keeping the heart from sin to keeping the head from error. As the breastplate of righteousness is a spiritual *heart* protector, the helmet of salvation is a spiritual *head* protector.

2. This covering of salvation is not *put on* as the other coverings have been, but it is to be *taken*—that is, this gift of God is to be *received or accepted.* "But as many as received Him, to them He gave the right to become children of God, to those who believe in His name" (John 1:12).

This new piece of armor is the *helmet of salvation.* The head of the soldier was among the principal parts to be defended, as on it the deadliest strokes might fall, and it is the head that commands the whole body. That is where the helmet, the soldier's valuable defensive armor, comes in. The head is the seat of the mind. Covered by the hope of eternal life, it will not receive false doctrine or give way to Satan's temptations to despair.[3]

infuse (in FYOOZ) : to cause to be permeated with something (as a principle or quality) that alters usually for the better

What is the *truth* about salvation?

True Salvation Is . . .

✦ *Exclusive—Salvation can be attained only by God's grace through faith in Jesus Christ.* "For by grace you have been saved through faith, and that not of yourselves; it is the gift of God, not of works, lest anyone should boast" (Ephesians 2:8–9).

✦ *Extensive—All things become new.* "Therefore, if anyone is in Christ, he is a new creation; old things have passed away; behold, all things have become new" (2 Corinthians 5:17).

If you travel with Student Leadership to Israel, you will visit the Garden Tomb, the site that many believe is the tomb where Christ was buried. Approaching the grave, peace will fill you because as you look inside, you will be reminded of the power of the truth of salvation.

Because Christ makes *all things new,* He has changed our lives. We can no longer go back to using old excuses about habits and choices in our lives. When you begin to see yourself as Christ sees you—as a new creation—you can have the freedom to become enthusiastic about the future rather than remain a slave to the past.

✦ *The chance to live again by faith.* "And you He made alive, who were dead in trespasses and sins" (Ephesians 2:1).

Salvation Is a Big Deal!
You may have grown up in the church hearing about salvation and eternal life. Never let it become routine to you. Never get over the wonder of transforming salvation.

Paul never got over his salvation experience. One hour he was persecuting Christians, and the next he was asking Christ, "What do You want me to do?"

In the Garden of Gethsemane, Jesus prayed, *"nevertheless, not as I will, but as You will,"* (Matthew 26:39). Salvation gives us the power to surrender our will as Christ did and ask, "What is Your will for my life today?"

This week pray Matthew 26:39 and trust God to work an amazing work in you.

Hold onto your personal salvation experience, whether it was eight years ago or yesterday. When we fully understand salvation and we allow the Holy Spirit to be real in our lives, then we are covered with the power of genuine salvation.

Write here or in your journal just a few sentences about an experience with Christ. Go over this often as you thank God for calling you personally to Himself.

The *helmet of salvation* protects our minds so that we do not become disoriented when assaulted by spiritual warfare.

diffuse (di FYOOZ): to pour out and permit or cause to spread freely; to extend, scatter

Kathy Hanegraaff gave birth to a tiny six-week-old fetus. The baby died instantly, but as she looked lovingly on the little form, a peace came over her. Kathy named the baby *Grace* because she said, "God has answered my prayers and has given me His grace. He has shown me that I didn't lose our baby. I know exactly where she is."[4] In a moment of deep personal despair, the hope of eternal life gave Kathy the strength, peace, and grace she needed.

The *helmet of salvation* causes us to look at life from an eternal point of view.

The Helmet of Salvation Blunts the Blow of Death

Satan wielded the sword of death with devastating fury.

✦ He butchered Job's livestock.

✦ He murdered Job's legacy.

✦ If God had permitted him to do so, he would have snuffed out Job's life.

The devil's devastation was so complete that even Job's wife had lost all perspective.

Job refused to look at the temporary and kept his point of view in the eternal. Having received the helmet of salvation, he was empowered to declare, "For I know that my Redeemer lives, and He shall stand at last on the earth; and after my skin is destroyed, this I know, that in my flesh I shall see God, whom I shall see for myself, and my eyes shall behold, and not another. How my heart yearns within me!" (Job 19:25–27).

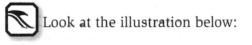 Look at the illustration below:

Although the demands and distresses of everyday life can make some problems seem to last forever, the truth is our lives are so very short in the light of eternity. James compared our lives to a "mist that appears for a little while and then vanishes" (James 4:14 NIV). Whether you live twenty years or ninety years, the window is small compared to the vastness of eternity. Spend some time this week contemplating the illustration: how will the reality of this time line affect the choices you make and how you choose to spend your time and energy?

What is ONE THING you could change—complaining, worry, procrastination, etc.—that would help you to move into an "eternal" state of mind?

_____

_____

_____

The Helmet of Salvation Protects from the Disorienting Blow of Doubt

Developing the habit of thanking God daily for salvation keeps gratitude fresh in our minds and its power close at hand, ready for any attacks on our faith.

Believe God is who He says He is:

+ *Unconditional Lover of my soul.* What can separate us from the love of Christ? Nothing! (Romans 8:31).

+ *All-powerful.* "He is able to do more than we can ask or imagine" (Ephesians 3:20).

+ *The One who holds my times in His hand.* "My times are in Your hand" (Psalm 31:15).

Remember Job's declaration:

✦ "'Shall we indeed accept good from God, and shall we not accept adversity?' In all this Job did not sin with his lips" (Job 2:10).

Suppose you pray and pray, but your friend or family member is not healed. Or suppose you work and work to be elected on the school council, but you do not win. As people come to you and ask, "Why didn't God answer your prayers?" will you be able to speak in faith as Job did?

_____

_____

_____

Why or why not?

_____

_____

_____

> There is no body in the tomb. Christ has risen; He has risen indeed! To receive genuine salvation is to receive victory over death. "He will swallow up death forever, And the Lord GOD will wipe away tears from all faces" (Isaiah 25:8).

GROUP DISCUSSION

Do you think some Christians are embarrassed to admit that sometimes God does not answer our prayers as we would like Him to? Do we have the faith to announce to others that we trust God regardless of how things look at the moment?

The Helmet of Salvation Blunts the Devastating Blow of Disappointment

When bad or tragic things happen, waves of fear tend to sweep away all perspective. We are plagued by the possibilities that life will be forever changed in some horrific way. Yet, as Christians, we can look to the promise of salvation to ease our doubts and drive away our dread of the unknown. God gives us a glimpse of glory. This life here on earth is not the end of the story. There is more!

That ultimately was the perspective of Job. The certainty of salvation not only assured him that in his flesh he would see God, but it assured him that in his flesh he would once again see his children, who were also believers.

 List one major disappointment you are currently facing or that you faced in the past:

_____

_____

_____

Now use the points above to pray through that hurt.

"Lord, guide my mind and help me to see the situation from an eternal point of view. I know You will work this for my good. I thank You for saving me and for the hope that is ahead. Heal this hurt by helping me to pray for and love others, by helping me to trust You with every moment of my life, by helping me to believe that You love me and want the best for me."

Life after death is not a crutch or a cop-out; it is a certainty. As Christians, we stake our lives on the hope of eternity when our corruptible bodies will take on incorruption (1 Corinthians 15:42).

[FUSE BOX]

Never "get over" your personal salvation.

The *helmet of salvation:*

✦ guards our minds and grants us perspective;

✦ allows us to take our eyes off the present and fix them on the future;

✦ enables us to look beyond our sorrow and see the promise of salvation;

✦ heals our hearts when nothing else will.

PRIVATE WORLD DEVOTIONS

MONDAY: See it. Read the surrounding passages or chapter for the Key Scripture so that you can get an understanding of the background and context. This helps you to really *see* the verse.

TUESDAY: Hear it. Read the daily Key Scripture and/or surrounding passage out loud, putting your name in, if applicable. For example, <u>John</u> *can do all things through Christ. Thieves have come to destroy* <u>John</u>, *but Jesus has come that* <u>John</u> *might have eternal life.*

WEDNESDAY: Write it. Write the verse and then what it says about:

✦ *Others:* Respond, serve, and love as Jesus would.

✦ *Me:* Specific attitudes, choices, or habits.

✦ *God:* His love, mercy, holiness, peace, joy, etc.

PRIVATE WORLD JOURNAL

I am grateful for—I praise You for—I am feeling—I am thinking—I need help with

PRIVATE WORLD DEVOTIONS *(Continued)*

THURSDAY: Memorize it. Take the verse with you—write it on a card or put it in your phone, iPod, or PDA. Go over it throughout the day so that it begins to *live* in your heart and mind.

FRIDAY: Pray it. Personalize the verse as you pray for yourself or for others or in praise to God. To pray is literally "to think about." Try thinking out loud or writing in your **PRIVATE WORLD JOURNAL.**

SATURDAY: Share it. Ask the Lord to bring someone to mind or in your path today who needs good news. Don't be shy—just let it out! Whether you IM, write, text, tell, or send it, the joy of God's Word will flow from your heart into theirs.

PRAYER REQUESTS

Date	Name	Need	Answer

PRIVATE WORLD JOURNAL

I am grateful for—I praise You for—I am feeling—I am thinking—I need help with

NOTES

CHAPTER 7

THE COVERING OF SCRIPTURE

KEY SCRIPTURE

And take . . . the sword of the Spirit,
which is the word of God.

—**Ephesians 6:17**

WHY KNOW IT?

✦ 58% of Christian teens believe the Bible to be "the actual word of God to be taken literally."[1]

✦ 38% believe the Bible to be "the inspired word of God, but not every verse should be taken literally."[2]

✦ The Bible is the world's best selling and most widely distributed book, with an estimated 2.5 billion copies sold since 1815. It has been translated into 2,233 languages and dialects.[3]

transfuse (trans FYOOZ); to cause to pass from one to another; transmit

The Word of God is living and powerful because it was divinely inspired. "All Scripture is given by inspiration of God, and is profitable for doctrine, for reproof, for correction, for instruction in righteousness" (2 Timothy 3:16).

*And take . . . the sword of the Spirit, which
is the word of God.* **—Ephesians 6:17**

Once again, we are told to *take* or *receive* this gift of covering.

As Christian writer William Gurnall has well said, "Throughout the ages the sword has been a most necessary part of the soldier's equipment and has been used more than any other weapon. A pilot without his chart, a student without his book, a solider without his sword— are all ridiculous. But above these, it is absurd to think of being a Christian without knowledge of God's Word and some skill to use this weapon."[4]

The sword of the Spirit is the Bible, furnished by the Holy Spirit, who inspired the writers of the Word of God, the two-edged sword, cutting both ways: convicting of sin and redemptive of sin.

In Matthew 4, we read about the ultimate spiritual battle. Jesus fasted forty days and forty nights, and the Scripture says that "afterward He was hungry" (v. 2). Alone, hungry, and tired, Satan sensed Jesus's vulnerability, and he was poised and ready to strike. He seized the moment, telling Jesus, "If You are the Son of God, command that these stones become bread" (Matthew 4:3).

Jesus might well have responded by unveiling His divine glory, but He didn't. Instead, He took up the sword of the Spirit. Jesus replied, "It is written, 'Man shall not live by bread alone, but by every word that proceeds from the mouth of God'" (Matthew 4:4).

Next, Satan challenged Jesus by throwing a Scripture back at him, saying, "If You are the Son of God, throw Yourself down. For it is written: 'He shall give His angels charge over you,' and, 'In their hands they shall bear you up, lest you dash your foot against a stone'" (Matthew 4:6).

Jesus could have whispered, "Help!" and God would have sent twelve legions of angels; but He didn't. He took up the sword of the Spirit and replied, "It is written again, 'You shall not tempt the LORD your God'" (Matthew 4:7).

In desperation, the devil took Jesus to the summit of a high mountain and showed Him the kingdoms of the world and their splendor. He said, "All these things I will give You if You will fall down and worship me" (Matthew 4:9).

Excuse me? Satan, the deceiver, will give the kingdoms of the world to Jesus, the Creator? I don't think so! Do you see what was really being offered here? Satan was saying to Jesus, "Give up that cross and dying for those people. Come and rule with me. It will be easy, pleasurable, and without sacrifice."

Jesus said, "No way!" He could have blinded the devil with the brilliance of His intellect, but He didn't. He took up the sword of the Spirit and proclaimed truth. "Away with you, Satan! For it is written, 'You shall worship the LORD your God, and Him only you shall serve'" (Matthew 4:10).

infuse (in FYOOZ)'; to cause to be permeated with something (as a principle or quality) that alters usually for the better

How Can We Prove That the Bible Is the Word of God?

The evidence for the divine inspiration of the Bible can be organized into four categories, each represented by one of the letters in the acronym M-A-P-S. This acronym should be easy to remember, because most Bibles have maps in the back. Just like we need maps to guide us through unfamiliar places, we need MAPS to guide us in our defense of the reliability of the Word of God.

M—Manuscript Evidence

Many people treat the Bible as if it is just another ancient text. The truth is that the Bible is in a class by itself when it comes to its historical reliability.

The historical accuracy of the Scriptures is indeed in a class by itself, far superior to other ancient texts. One of the primary ways that historians determine the reliability of ancient texts is called the bibliographic test. According to this test, the more manuscripts, or copies, we have of a book, and the closer the dating of those manuscripts are to the original writing, the more reliable the book. Using this test, the Bible has been shown to be vastly more reliable than any other work of ancient literature.

For example, *The Annals of Imperial Rome,* written by Tacitus about AD 116, is considered a reliable history of Rome, even though the first six books exist today in only one manuscript, dated to AD 850; books eleven through sixteen are in another manuscript copied in the eleventh century AD; and books seven through ten are lost. And second only to the Bible in terms of manuscript evidence is Homer's *Iliad,* which was written around 800 BC and of which we have fewer than 650 manuscripts, dating to the second and third centuries AD.

Compare that to the Old Testament, of which we have more than 14,000 manuscripts and portions, the earliest dating to 200–250 BC (the Old Testament was completed around 400 BC); and the New Testament, of which we have over 5,300 manuscripts and portions, the earliest portions being dated to an astounding sixty years or so from the original writings!

The earliest full manuscript of the New Testament is dated to around AD 350, less than three hundred years from the original writings. If we can trust Tacitus's accounts of Roman history and believe that Homer's *Iliad* has been preserved over time, then we can certainly trust that the Bible has been accurately transmitted over time without tampering.

A—Archaeological Evidence

While the manuscript evidence assures us that the Bible has not been altered over time and points to God's sovereign preservation of the Bible throughout history, external evidences such as the testimony of secular historians and archaeological confirmations of the biblical record continue to demonstrate that the Old and New Testaments are historically accurate and trustworthy texts.

Dr. Nelson Glueck, probably the greatest modern authority on Israeli archeology, has said, "No archeological discovery has ever controverted a Biblical reference. Scores of archeological findings have been made which confirm in clear outline or in exact detail historical statements in the Bible. And, by the same token, proper evaluation of Biblical descriptions has often led to amazing discoveries."[5]

Consider the following examples of how archeology has proven the Bible trustworthy:

✦ Explorers recently discovered a skeleton of a man in a burial cave near the Nablus road outside of Jerusalem. This skeleton demonstrates the accuracy of the biblical description of Roman crucifixion—the man's open arms had been nailed to a cross bar, and one large nail had nailed his feet to the cross through both heels; his shins also appeared to be broken, corroborating the biblical explanation that Roman soldiers would break the legs of the crucified person to ensure death.

✦ For years biblical critics, relying on a lack of historical references to Belshazzar and on the testimony of Greek historians who recorded

Nabonidus as the last king of Babylon, claimed that Belshazzar was a fictional personality invented by the biblical author Daniel. These critics were later silenced when inscriptions were uncovered that identified Belshazzar as Nabonidus's son, whom he left in charge of Babylon while he was away for an extended period of time.

✦ One of the most well-known New Testament examples concerns the books of Luke and Acts. A biblical skeptic, Sir William Ramsay, trained as an archaeologist, set out to disprove the historical reliability of this portion of the New Testament. However, through his painstaking Mediterranean archaeological trips, he became converted as one after another of the historical statements of Luke were proven accurate.

This list is only the tip of the iceberg of archaeological finds that demonstrate the historical reliability of the Bible. "Truly with every turn of the archaeologist's spade we continue to see evidence for the trustworthiness of Scripture."[6]

P—Prophecy Fulfilled

The prophetic evidences for the Bible's divine inspiration are overwhelming. Anyone with an open mind will be compelled by the Bible's fulfilled prophecies to consider its veracity and its central message of redemption in Jesus Christ.

The Bible contains an abundance of specific prophecies concerning the birth, life, death, and resurrection of Jesus Christ—some of which were made well over two thousand years prior to His birth. Learn these facts so that you can use them in defending the Word of God:

- ✦ Christ would be a descendant of Abraham (Genesis 12:1–3; 17:19; Matthew 1:1–2; Acts 3:25).

- ✦ He would be from the tribe of Judah (Genesis 49:10; Matthew 1:1–2) and the house of David (Psalm 110:1; Matthew 1:1).

- ✦ He would be born in Bethlehem (Micah 5:2; Matthew 2:1, 6) of a virgin (Isaiah 7:1–4; Matthew 1:18–23).

- ✦ He would be betrayed for thirty pieces of silver (Zechariah 11:12; Matthew 26:14–16).

- ✦ His hands and feet would be pierced (Psalm 22:16; John 20:25). It is noteworthy that this last prediction was made long before crucifixion was invented as a form of capital punishment by the Persians and a thousand years before it was made common by the Romans!

- ✦ Christ would be crucified with transgressors (Isaiah 53:12; Matthew 27:38).

- ✦ None of His bones would be broken (Exodus 12:46; Psalm 34:20; John 19:33–37).

- ✦ The soldiers would gamble for His clothes (Psalm 22:18; Matthew 27:35).

- ✦ He would be buried among the rich (Isaiah 53:9; Matthew 27:57–60).

These prophecies do not deal with vague generalities (as is so often the case with modern-day "prophets" and psychics); they are specific and verifiable. Each was literally fulfilled down to the smallest detail in the person of Jesus Christ.

And Jesus Himself made predictions about the future that were verifiable by His disciples because they were to be fulfilled in their generation. For example, Jesus predicted His own death and resurrection (John 2:19–22). Jesus also predicted the destruction of Jerusalem and the Jewish temple (Luke 21)—a prophecy that was fulfilled when the Roman army destroyed the temple and the city in AD 70.[7]

S—Statistical Probability

More than forty authors wrote one consistent Book. Although it is a collection of 66 books written by 40 different human authors in three different languages (Hebrew, Aramaic, and Greek) over a period of 1,500 years, the Bible is unified and consistent.

One theme occurs throughout. God's great work in the creation and redemption of all things, through His only Son, the Lord Jesus Christ, is woven throughout the pages of both the Old and New Testaments. More than forty authors over thousands of years, and still one central message.

How is that possible? The individual writers had no idea that their message would eventually be assembled into one Book, yet each work fits perfectly into place with a unique purpose as a component of the whole.

This statistically improbable unity cannot be explained by chance or by mere human design; the Bible is a divinely inspired work.

The Bible Changes Lives

While this last category is not included in the MAPS acronym, as it is less scientific at its core, it is nevertheless accurate and genuine.

Men and women over the ages have been changed, empowered, healed, and forever transformed through the writings of the Word of God. (What about your testimony?)

Rich and poor, prince and pauper, the intellectual and the simple-minded, all races, backgrounds, and walks of life have been changed by its power. No other book has ever held such universal appeal, brought such lasting effects, and continued in print over so many generations.

Take the time to organize a goal sheet in your planner:

Why? To be able to *give an answer* when asked about the truth of God's Word.

What? To know the facts about the divine inspiration and writing of the Bible.

When? Decide that this week, you will:

Study _____ a day over a period of _____ weeks

Study _____ a week over a period of _____ months

How? Break it down into manageable bites. Use M-A-P-S to guide you:

1. *Manuscript Evidence*

2. *Archaeological Evidence*

3. *Prophecy Fulfilled* (You don't have to know them all by heart. Keep them available.)

4. *Statistical Probability*

   ✦ Author backgrounds and time lines.

   ✦ Understand the Bible's unifying theme.

5. Be able to tell testimonies, including yours, of a transformed life.

This covering of Scripture is not only a Book in our homes or in our hands. It is a living covering, one we must learn to use with precision and accuracy on the battlefield of life.

What is ONE THING specifically that you are tempted by and struggle with? Admit it. Face it. Write it here.

_____

_____

_____

This week, find at least three verses that you can keep on cards in your planner or pocket or car that can be stated as an "It is written" answer to Satan's temptations:

1. _____

2. _____

3. _____

Arm Yourself with Scripture

As Jesus armed Himself with the sword of the Spirit, the Word of God, so must we.

Armed with reason alone, we stand defenseless before an intellectually superior enemy, one who has studied us thoroughly and is intimately acquainted with all of our vulnerabilities.

Armed with the sword of the Spirit, we are a terror to Satan and can stand strong in the face of his fiercest temptations.

diffuse (di FYOOZ) : to pour out and permit or cause to spread freely; to extend, scatter

It is not enough to be acquainted with the Word; you must *know* this Word. "Your word I have hidden in my heart, that I might not sin against You!" (Psalm 119:11).

Charles Spurgeon says, "Let it never be said that God has recorded truths in His word that you have not read. Study the word and work out its meaning. Go deep into the spirit of inspiration. He gets the most gold who digs the deepest in this mine. The deeper you go under the Spirit's guidance, the larger the reward for your toil."[8]

How much time do you spend not just reading, but *studying*, God's Word? Determine to set aside enough time in your Private World to study one day a week.

Which day?

_____

_____

_____

Too many students today approach the Bible as if it can mean different things to different people. And when asked about the meaning of a passage of Scripture, rather than reading each passage in its context, they simply read a verse and then look up from the Bible and say something like, "To me, this verse means . . . "

Every verse in the Bible has an objective meaning that is true for everyone. We must not let ourselves be satisfied with mere opinions about the meaning of a passage; we must diligently study to discover the truth of every passage.

Use the acronym L-I-G-H-T-S to help you understand the principles for interpreting Scripture accurately. These LIGHTS will help you mine the depths of the covering of Scripture, a necessary piece of the spiritual armor of every warrior of God.

L*iteral principle of biblical interpretation*—Interpret the Word in its most obvious and literal sense, according to its genre and context. The Bible contains poetry, prophecy, biography, and history; and each genre uses language in different ways and must be interpreted accordingly. The books of the Bible should be interpreted using the rules of interpretation for any other literature, guided by the Holy Spirit.

I*llumination principle*—God wants you to understand truth! That is why He gave you the Bible. Ask the Lord to help you understand His Word as you apply sound principles of interpretation to the text. As you diligently apply these principles of biblical interpretation the Spirit will faithfully illumine the true meaning of the text. His intention is never darkness, for He commands us to *walk in the light.* "Now we have received, not the spirit of the world, but the Spirit who is from God, that we might know the things that have been freely given to us by God" (1 Corinthians 2:12).

G*rammar principle*—Scripture must always be interpreted in accordance with typical rules of grammar, using:

+ semantics: the meaning of words;

+ syntax: the way words are put together to form phrases;

+ style: a distinctive manner of expression.

H*istorical principle*—Understanding of the biblical text is enhanced when studied along with the customs, culture, and historical context of biblical times. Though the Bible was written *for* us, it was not written *to* us. To understand the meaning of Scripture, we must understand the mind-sets of the original audiences to whom the words of Scripture were written. Don't be a lazy student. There are many free Internet sources available to teach you these biblical backgrounds, including www.equip.org. (Warning: there are also many untrustworthy sources on the Internet. Surf with caution!)

Get in there, swim around, and enjoy God's Word, His gift to you.

Teaching principle—It has been said that to truly own a truth, one must teach it or share it with others. Jesus confirmed this when He told His disciples, "Go therefore and make disciples of all the nations, baptizing them in the name of the Father and of the Son and of the Holy Spirit, teaching them to observe all things that I have commanded you" (Matthew 28:19–20). The writer to the Hebrews emphasized this point, writing, "In fact, though by this time you ought to be teachers, you need someone to teach you the elementary truths of God's word all over again" (Hebrews 5:12 NIV).

To be entrusted with such a valuable and influential task as a Christian requires that we teach the Bible carefully and accurately, without regard to opinion or culture bias. As James warned, "Not many of you should presume to be teachers, my brothers, because you know that we who teach will be judged more strictly" (James 3:1 NIV). Do not take this responsibility lightly!

Before the Lord can trust you with teaching a group, He must see you faithful to share on a daily basis and one-on-one. Ask Him for opportunity to share—in the halls, on the job, in your home or neighborhood, even in your youth group. Everyone has questions. The Bible has the answers. Be the delivery guy/girl. "Do your best to present yourself to God as one approved, a workman who does not need to be ashamed and who correctly handles the word of truth" (2 Timothy 2:15 NIV).

Scriptural harmony—Individual passages of Scripture, when interpreted correctly, will always harmonize with Scripture as a whole. One text can never be pulled out of context in order to be interpreted in such a way as to conflict with other passages.

This is where many students get into trouble. They make the Bible say what they want it to say for their circumstance instead of just taking God at His Word. He means just what He says. Remember, context is key!

In the next chapter, we will learn about the covering of a lifestyle of prayer. Using practical visualization techniques, we will discover how to know the Word through consistent, deliberate memorization of the Scriptures.

Prepare your heart this week. Ask God to forgive sin in your life and to give you a spiritual tenacity to learn about the Word and how to effectively use it.

FUSE BOX

It is not enough to have the Word of God in our homes or in our hands. We must deftly wield it on the battlefield of life.

NOTES

PRIVATE WORLD DEVOTIONS

MONDAY: See it. Read the surrounding passages or chapter for the Key Scripture so that you can get an understanding of the background and context. This helps you to really *see* the verse.

TUESDAY: Hear it. Read the daily Key Scripture and/or surrounding passage out loud, putting your name in, if applicable. For example, <u>John</u> *can do all things through Christ. Thieves have come to destroy* <u>John</u>, *but Jesus has come that* <u>John</u> *might have eternal life.*

WEDNESDAY: Write it. Write the verse and then what it says about:

- ✦ *Others:* Respond, serve, and love as Jesus would.
- ✦ *Me:* Specific attitudes, choices, or habits.
- ✦ *God:* His love, mercy, holiness, peace, joy, etc.

PRIVATE WORLD JOURNAL

I am grateful for—I praise You for—I am feeling—I am thinking—I need help with

PRIVATE WORLD DEVOTIONS *(Continued)*

THURSDAY: Memorize it. Take the verse with you—write it on a card or put it in your phone, iPod, or PDA. Go over it throughout the day so that it begins to *live* in your heart and mind.

FRIDAY: Pray it. Personalize the verse as you pray for yourself or for others or in praise to God. To pray is literally "to think about." Try thinking out loud or writing in your **PRIVATE WORLD JOURNAL.**

SATURDAY: Share it. Ask the Lord to bring someone to mind or in your path today who needs good news. Don't be shy—just let it out! Whether you IM, write, text, tell, or send it, the joy of God's Word will flow from your heart into theirs.

PRAYER REQUESTS

Date	Name	Need	Answer

PRIVATE WORLD JOURNAL

I am grateful for—I praise You for—I am feeling—I am thinking—I need help with

NOTES

CHAPTER 8

THE COVERING OF A LIFESTYLE OF PRAYER

KEY SCRIPTURE

Praying always with all prayer and supplication in the Spirit, being watchful to this end with all perseverance and supplication for all the saints.
—Ephesians 6:18

WHY KNOW IT?

✦ When asked about the desires they have for their future, 84% of teens value close, personal friendships, 83% desire one marriage partner for life, and 66% wanted a close, personal relationship with God.[1]

✦ When asked, "How do you feel about the amount of expressions of faith and prayer by political leaders?" 21% surveyed said they felt there was "too much" expression, and 41% said "too little."[2]

transfuse (trans FYOOZ): to cause to pass from one to another; transmit

As you walk the bridge toward independence in life, you must also move forward into a personal, genuine prayer life. How do you do this?

Stop seeing prayer as merely a means of bringing our requests.

Start seeing prayer as an opportunity to build a relationship with the Lover of our souls.

Praying always with all prayer and supplication in the Spirit, being watchful to this end with all perseverance and supplication for all the saints. —**Ephesians 6:18**

Prayer is not a mere piece of the covering; it is much more than that. Prayer is indelibly woven into each piece of the covering. It is to the armor what oxygen is to the lungs: the foundation, the first principle of spiritual warfare.

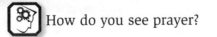

infuse (in FYOOZ) ; to cause to be permeated with something (as a principle or quality) that alters usually for the better

"Praying always . . . "

When you understand that to pray to God is to communicate with Him, to build a relationship with Him, to listen for His voice, then you begin to understand prayer.

Just as you must breathe oxygen for physical life, you must spiritually breathe through prayer for spiritual life.

How do you see prayer?

✦ As a necessary but unpleasant job;

✦ As a task on your "to do" list;

✦ As an optional part of the Christian life;

✦ As a necessary part of a relationship with Christ;

✦ As the opportunity to have a genuine, intimate relationship with God.

> "Every great movement of God can be traced to a kneeling figure."
> -D.L. Moody (1837–1899)

Perhaps you have believed all of these at one time or another.

This *praying always* is not staying on your knees or in a dark room 24–7, but it is consistent communication with God.

Imagine for a moment that your best friend doesn't speak to you for two days or so. How would that make you feel?

_____

_____

Suppose you see him/her in the hallway, and your friend only speaks a few sentences before leaving. Would that begin to change the closeness of that relationship?

_____

_____

Now think about how intensely and deeply God loves you. How must He feel when you give Him just a few words?

_____

_____

_____

" . . . in the Spirit . . . "

To pray *in the Spirit* is to pray for the will and purposes of God.

Powerless prayer begins by asking for your will instead of God's. When you end a prayer with "amen," you are in effect saying, "May it be so in accordance with the will of God."

When you pray:

+ *Conform to God's will.* Do not plead for God to conform to your will.

+ *Recognize the sovereignty of God over every detail of life.* There is great peace in knowing that God has every detail of our lives under control.

+ *Listen to the living Word of God—that is, the Scripture.* One of the most amazing aspects of the sword is that it is alive and active, not dead and dull. Indeed, God still speaks today through the mystery of His Word.

Satan's foremost strategy of seduction is to disguise himself as an angel of enlightenment (2 Corinthians 11:14), and his slickest slogan is "Feel; don't think."

God's Spirit, on the other hand, illumines our minds so that we may understand what He has freely given us; and this is not dependent on our emotions.

" . . . with all perseverance and supplication . . . "

Perseverance is to persist against all odds.

+ In a culture that does not understand or honor the glory of God, we are to continually offer Him honor and praise.

+ When a need is evident, we are to pray in strength.

The Prayer of Jesus

In what is called the Lord's Prayer, Jesus outlined effective prayer. If you are having trouble staying on track in your prayer life—and many of us do—follow the pattern that Jesus gave His disciples. Anyone can do it; every Christian must do it. The covering that God provides is not complete until we develop a genuine prayer life.

1. *Begin with honoring the glory of God.* "Our Father in heaven, hallowed be Your name" (Matthew 6:9).

2. *Open your heart to conform to God's will.* "Your kingdom come. Your will be done on earth as it is in heaven" (Matthew 6:10).

3. *Ask God to meet your needs that day.* "Give us this day our daily bread" (Matthew 6:11).

4. *Daily confess sin and petition for forgiveness.* "And forgive us our debts, as we forgive our debtors" (Matthew 6:12).

5. *Pray for protection.* "And do not lead us into temptation, but deliver us from the evil one" (Matthew 6:13).

6. *Finish with praise.* "For Yours is the kingdom and the power and the glory forever. Amen" (Matthew 6:13).

> Prayer—the easiest thing to do—just talk to God!
>
> Prayer—the hardest thing to do—I don't know what to say!
>
> Which one of these represents you?

Select one of the previous six steps, and then write one sentence of prayer that corresponds to it.

Step:

_____

_____

_____

Prayer:

_____

_____

_____

Keeping a prayer journal can be a very exciting part of your life. Writing your prayers allows you to focus your feelings and emotions. Dating your petitions allows you to go back and thank God for what He has done for you and others. It gives you the faith to continue to pray and trust Him. You can use the steps above, write your own psalms of praise, or freely express your praise, thanksgivings, and requests to God.

Whether you use an inexpensive spiral notebook or a beautifully decorated and bound journal, what's inside will be of great value.

"Praying . . . for all the saints."

Note that in Ephesians 6:18, we are told to pray "for all the saints."

Who are the *saints?* Every believer, even you! You are not a saint because you are sinless, but because you believe in Christ and have received His righteousness from God.

Imagine what would happen if your youth group, instead of praying as lone soldiers, were to begin praying together as a mighty army for God, praying for one another and for other believers in your community and around the world. The focus on praying for others is life changing!

You will remember in chapter 5, "The Covering of Faith," we read that Job lost his family, his possessions, and even his health in a period of great sorrow. After forty-two chapters of suffering and questioning, peace takes over, and God restored everything Job lost twice over. What caused the change? Look at this: "The LORD restored Job's losses when he prayed for his friends. Indeed the LORD gave Job twice as much as he had before" (Job 42:10).

> Now the LORD came and stood and called as at other times, "Samuel! Samuel!" And Samuel answered, "Speak, for Your servant hears."
> —1 Samuel 3:10

Job's suffering ended when he stopped praying for himself and began to pray for others! A powerful prayer life persistently petitions on behalf of others and infuses us with confident faith.

If this prayer *in the Spirit* is to conform us to the will of God, then we must use the Word of God in our prayer time. There is great power available when we meditate on Scripture.

If you are reading the Word, but not experiencing a vibrant prayer life;

if you are praying words, but not thriving in your quiet time;

Meditation on the Word of God is the missing link.

It's better to read a single passage and meditate on it than to read an entire book of the Bible and not think deeply about it.

Choose ONE THING to focus on this week that you have learned about the covering. Write it here:

_____

_____

_____

Scripture feeds meditation;

meditation gives food to our prayers.

Commit to five minutes each day this week to meditate on this truth. *What time* will you do this?

_____

_____

Prayer is only as inspired as our intake of Scripture. This living Word of God must fill your mind and heart.

diffuse (di FYOOZ): to pour out and permit or cause to spread freely; to extend, scatter

Ultimately, only when we put on the whole armor of God are we able to stand against the wiles of the devil. To put on the covering as a lifestyle assumes not only that you understand what the full armor of God represents, but that you are able to remember each piece of the armor as well.

Meditating on Scripture leads to memorizing the Scripture as your own dear possession.

Knowing the Scripture gives you power over temptation because you are able to remember God's Word in the face of temptation as Jesus did:

✦ "He answered and said, 'It is written, "Man shall not live by bread alone, but by every word that proceeds from the mouth of God"'" (Matthew 4:4).

✦ "Jesus said to him, 'It is written again, "You shall not tempt the LORD your God"'" (Matthew 4:7).

✦ "Then Jesus said to him, 'Away with you, Satan! For it is written, "You shall worship the LORD your God, and Him only you shall serve"'" (Matthew 4:10).

Here's the powerful result: "Then the devil left Him, and behold, angels came and ministered to Him" (Matthew 4:11).

All of memory can be reduced to the process of making associations—a name with a face, a state with a capital, or a chapter in the Bible with its content. If the pieces of information are correctly associated, when you think of one, you will think of the other.

GROUP DISCUSSION

Work together to imagine associations that will help you to memorize the pieces of the covering. Following you will find some ideas to get you started, but brainstorm together to come up with unique or even silly ideas. Keep in mind that the more unusual the association, the easier it is to remember!

Are you ready?

Truth: As you put on your belt each morning, imagine that your belt buckle is made out of a giant tooth. As your waist is the center of your body, so truth is central to the full armor of God. Without it, the covering that protects you from the devil's schemes simply crumples to the ground, leaving you naked and vulnerable.

Associate: Truth—giant tooth.

Visualize: Belt of truth—truth tooth.

Truth can be symbolized by _____
_____.

As a Christian leader, Truth should be foremost on your mind. Study God's Word daily and hide it in your heart so that you can lead others to understand Truth.

Righteousness: As you button your shirt or blouse, picture yourself putting on the breastplate of righteousness. Place your hand over your heart for a moment as you remember that truth must join with righteousness in order to give you the moral authority to speak.

Associate: Righteousness—right hand.

Visualize: Breastplate of righteousness—right hand over heart.

The breastplate can be symbolized by _____
_____.

Peace: As you put on your shoes each day, remember that the priceless material with which God has fitted

THE COVERING OF
A LIFESTYLE OF PRAYER

your feet for readiness in spiritual warfare is nothing less than the gospel of peace. With your feet fashioned with the readiness that comes from the gospel of peace, you can stand firm in distress, disease, destruction, and even death.

Associate: Peace—peas.

Visualize: Feet shod with gospel of peace—peas in your shoes.

Peace can be symbolized by _____

_____.

As you walk the halls of school or church, meet new people, or talk with friends, be aware that everyone wants peace in their lives. Share freely about what God is doing in your life and heart, not in judgment or smugness, but with enthusiasm. Then others will see the peace of God in you and be drawn to a relationship with Christ.

Faith: Every time you lift your hand (brush teeth, eat breakfast, pick out clothes, etc.), think of the shield of faith. The ancient shield enveloped the body and faith envelops your entire being. When Satan attacks your head, the hand of faith holds fast to truth. When Satan attacks your heart, the hand of faith holds fast to righteousness. In fact, it might well be said that the shield of faith is the apex of your armor. It is the grace "with which you can extinguish all the flaming arrows of the evil one."

PICTURE THIS! It has been accurately said that one best remembers what is first visualized. As you learn to make conscious associations through mental pictures, you will soon discover that you can recall information quickly and easily. Once the information is firmly rooted in your mind, the visual associations are no longer necessary.

Associate: Faith—face.

Visualize: Shield of faith—hand covering your face.

Faith can be symbolized by _____
_____.

Salvation: As you comb your hair, imagine you are putting on the helmet of salvation. Just as the breastplate of righteousness is your spiritual heart protector, the helmet of salvation is your spiritual head protector. It is the covering that protects your mind so that you do not become disoriented in the throes of spiritual warfare.

Associate: Hair—helmet.

Visualize: Helmet of salvation—hair, hat, or wig.

Salvation can be symbolized by _____
_____.

Scripture: From this day forward, as you pick up your Bible, may "the sword of the Spirit, which is the Word of God," flash through your mind. Armed with the puny sword of reason, you stand impotent before an enemy who has studied you thoroughly and is intimately acquainted with all your vulnerabilities. Armed with the sword of the Spirit, however, you are a terror to Satan and can stand strong in the face of his fiercest temptations.

Associate: Bible—sword.

Visualize: Bible—sword with words written on it.

Scripture can be symbolized by _____
_____.

Prayer: Finally, each time you open your eyes in the morning or close them at the end of the day, remember that prayer is firing the winning shot. Prayer is not merely a piece of the armor; rather, it is the thread that weaves the covering into an exquisite tapestry. It is the given, the foundation, the first principle of God's plan to protect you from evil!

As you put on the covering of a lifestyle of prayer, you will experience God's supernatural protection in the invisible war. The goal is that you will one day be able to say: "I have fought the good fight, I have finished the race, I have kept the faith" (2 Timothy 4:7).

Associate: Prayer—hands folded.

Visualize: Closed eyes, open palms.

Prayer can be symbolized by _____ _____.

[FUSE BOX]

The key to supernatural protection in the invisible war is not found in *exorcising* demons, but in *exercising* spiritual disciplines.

PRIVATE WORLD DEVOTIONS

MONDAY: See it. Read the surrounding passages or chapter for the Key Scripture so that you can get an understanding of the background and context. This helps you to really *see* the verse.

TUESDAY: Hear it. Read the daily Key Scripture and/or surrounding passage out loud, putting your name in, if applicable. For example, <u>John</u> *can do all things through Christ. Thieves have come to destroy* <u>John</u>, *but Jesus has come that* <u>John</u> *might have eternal life.*

WEDNESDAY: Write it. Write the verse and then what it says about:

✦ *Others:* Respond, serve, and love as Jesus would.

✦ *Me:* Specific attitudes, choices, or habits.

✦ *God:* His love, mercy, holiness, peace, joy, etc.

PRIVATE WORLD JOURNAL

*I am grateful for—I praise You for—I am
feeling—I am thinking—I need help with*

PRIVATE WORLD DEVOTIONS (Continued)

THURSDAY: Memorize it. Take the verse with you—write it on a card or put it in your phone, iPod, or PDA. Go over it throughout the day so that it begins to *live* in your heart and mind.

FRIDAY: Pray it. Personalize the verse as you pray for yourself or for others or in praise to God. To pray is literally "to think about." Try thinking out loud or writing in your **PRIVATE WORLD JOURNAL.**

SATURDAY: Share it. Ask the Lord to bring someone to mind or in your path today who needs good news. Don't be shy—just let it out! Whether you IM, write, text, tell, or send it, the joy of God's Word will flow from your heart into theirs.

PRAYER REQUESTS

Date	Name	Need	Answer

PRIVATE WORLD JOURNAL

I am grateful for—I praise You for—I am feeling—I am thinking—I need help with

Notes

CHAPTER 1—CAN THE DEVIL MAKE YOU DO IT?

1. "Half of All Adults Say Their Faith Helped Them Personally Handle the 9-11 Aftermath," The Barna Group (3 September 2002). 15 August 2005. http://www.barna.org/FlexPage.aspx?Page = BarnaUpdate&BarnaUpdateID = 120.

2. David W. Moore, "Three in Four Americans Believe in Paranormal," The Gallup Organization (16 June 2005). http://poll.gallup.com/content/default.aspx?ci = 16915&pg = 1.

3. *The Usual Suspects* (Metro Goldwyn Mayer: 1995).

4. "Teens Evaluate Church-Based Ministry They Received As Children," The BarnaGroup (8 July 2003). 6 July 2005. http://www.barna.org/FlexPage.aspx?Page = BarnaUpdate&BarnaUpdate ID = 143.

5. C. S. Lewis, The *Screwtape Letters* (New York: MacMillan, 1961), Preface.

CHAPTER 2—THE BATTLE FOR YOUR MIND

1. Results for "spiritual warfare" and "demon," Amazon.com (accessed 10 January 2006)..

2. Charles Spurgeon, *Spiritual Warfare in a Believer's Life*, updated by Robert Hall (Lynnwood, Wash.: Emerald, 1993), 30.

3. Randy Alcorn, *Lord Foulgrin's Letters,* (Sisters, Ore.: Multnomah, 2000), 299.

CHAPTER 3—THE COVERING OF TRUTH AND RIGHTEOUSNESS

1. Google.com, s.v. "spiritual warfare," "eRumor" (accessed 10 January 2006).

2. "What Is the Response Time?" www.internettrafficreport.com (accessed 28 August 2005).

3. Adapted from quote attributed to Charles Haddon Spurgeon.

4. Os Guinness, *Time for Truth* (Grand Rapids: Baker, 2000), 79–80.

5. Merriam-Webster Online Dictionary, s.v. "truth." http://www.m-w.com/cgi-bin/dictionary?book = Dictionary&va = truth.

6. Merriam-Webster Online Dictionary, s.v. "righteousness." http://www.m-w.com/cgi-bin/dictionary?book = Dictionary&va = righteousness.

CHAPTER 4—THE COVERING OF PEACE

1. "Evangelism," The Barna Group, http://www.barna.org/FlexPage.aspx?Page = Topic&TopicID = 18 (accessed 10 January 2006).

2. Ibid.

3. M.G. Easton, *Illustrated Bible Dictionary*, 3rd ed. (Nashville: Thomas Nelson, 1987), s.v. "gospel."

4. C.H. Spurgeon, "Shoes for Pilgrims and Warriors," *The Sword and the Trowel*, November 1874.

5. Julie Ray, "U.S. Teens Walk Away from Anger," The Gallup Organization (12 April 2005). 1 August 2005. http://poll.gallup.com/content/default.aspx?CI = 15811.

CHAPTER 5—THE COVERING OF FAITH

1. "Teenagers and Spirituality," The Barna Group (1999). http://www.barna.org/FlexPage.aspx?Page = Topic&TopicID = 37.

2. Sandy, James M., Thomas Ashby Wills, Alison M. Yaeger, "Buffering Effect of Religiosity for Adolescent Substance Abuse," *Psychology of Addictive Behaviors* 17 (2003): 24–31.

3. William Gurnall, *The Christian in Complete Armour*, vol. 3. (Edinburgh, Great Britain: The Banner of Truth Trust, 1989 [originally published in 1662]), 30.

4. Lydia Saad, "Americans Familiar With, Fond of Billy Graham," The Gallup Organization (23 June 2005). 18 August 2005. http://poll.gallup.com/content/default.aspx?CI = 17029.

CHAPTER 6—THE COVERING OF SALVATION

1. "Americans Describe Their Views About Life After Death," The Barna Group (21 October 2003). http://www.barna.org/FlexPage. aspx?Page = BarnaUpdate&BarnaUpdateID = 150 (accessed 19 August 2005).

2. Ibid.

3. Robert Jamieson, A.R. Fausset, and David Brown, *Jamieson-Fausset-Brown Bible Commentary, s.v.* "Ephesians," http://biblecrosswalk. com/Commentaries/JamiesonFaussetBrown/jfb.cgi?book = eph.

4. Hank Hanegraaff, *The Covering* (Nashville: W Publishing Group, 2002), 78.

CHAPTER 7—THE COVERING OF SCRIPTURE

1. Albert Winesman, "Teens' Stance on the Word of God," The Gallup Organization (22 March 2005). http://poll.gallup.com/content/default.aspx?CI = 15313 (accessed 19 August 2005).

2. Ibid.

3. "Best Selling Non-fiction Book," Guinness Book of World Records. http://www.guinnessworldrecords.com.

4. William Gurnall, *The Christian in Complete Armour,* vol. 3. (Edinburgh, Great Britain: The Banner of Truth Trust, 1989 [originally published in 1662]), 222.

5. Henry Morris and Martin Clark, *The Bible Has the Answer* (El Cajon, Calif.: Master Books, 1987).

6. Hank Hanegraaff and Paul Maier, *The DaVinci Code: Fact or Fiction?* (Wheaton, Ill: Tyndale, 2004), 48.

7. Adapted from Hanegraaff and Maier, *The DaVinci Code: Fact or Fiction?,* 50.

8. Charles Spurgeon, *Spiritual Warfare in a Believer's Life,* updated by Robert Hall (Lynnwood, Wash.: Emerald, 1993), 174.

1. "Teenagers," The Barna Group, http://www.barna.org/FlexPage. aspx?Page = Topic&TopicID = 37 (accessed 11 January 2006).

2. Pew Research Center and the Pew Forum on Religion and Public Life, "Religion and Politics: Contention and Consensus," http://www.beliefnet.com/story/150/story_15007_1.html (accessed 11 January 2006).

ABOUT THE AUTHORS

Jay Strack, president and founder of Student Leadership University, is an inspiring and effective communicator, author, and minister. Acclaimed by leaders in the business world, religious affiliations, and education realms as a dynamic speaker, Jay has spoken to an estimated 15 million people in his 30 years of ministry. His versatile style has been presented across the country and in 22 countries, before government officials, corporate groups, numerous professional sports teams in the NFL, NBA, and MLB, to over 9,500 school assemblies, and at some 100 universities. Zig Ziglar calls Jay Strack, "entertaining, but powerful, inspiring and informative."

Hank Hanegraaff serves as president and chairman of the board of the California-based Christian Research Institute International (CRI). He also hosts CRI's "Bible Answer Man" program, which is broadcast daily across the United States and Canada. Hanegraaff came to faith in Jesus Christ as a result of examining the scientific evidence for creation, the resurrection of Jesus and the inspiration of Scriptures. Hanegraaff's book, *The F.A.C.E. that Demonstrates the Farce of Evolution* also won the 1999 Silver Medallion for excellence in the Christianity and Society category. Other book titles include *Counterfeit Revival, Christianity in Crisis, Resurrection, The Millennium Bug Debugged, Personal Witness Training: Your Handle on the Great Commission, Memory Dynamics: Your Untapped Resource for Spiritual Growth,* and *The Covering.* He is also a regular contributor to The Christian Research Journal and The Plain Truth Magazine. A popular conference speaker, he addresses churches, schools, and businesses worldwide. Hank lives in North Carolina with his wife, Kathy and their eight children.

The journey continues.

SLU201, SLU301, SLU401! – We kick it up a notch!

Student Leadership University believes you'll be the same person five years from now as you are today, except for...The places you go, The people you meet, The books you read. **201-Washington, D.C.** – Exclusive SLU 201 Level Two Sessions in Leadership, Worldview, and Behind the Scenes experiences give an in-depth look at the foundation of our country. **301-London-Paris-Normandy-Oxford** – Step off the plane and into history as we honor the past and learn to transform the future. **401-Rome-Athens-Ephesus-Florence-Pompeii** – Explore the days of ancient history and get inspired to Live a Legacy of Faith.

For more information call
Toll-free: 1-888-260-2900
www.studentleadership.net

Student Leadership
UNIVERSITY

CHRISTIAN RESEARCH INSTITUTE

The Christian Research Institute (CRI) exists to provide Christians worldwide with carefully researched information and well-reasoned answers that encourage them in their faith and equip them to intelligently represent it to people influenced by ideas and teachings that assault or undermine orthodox, biblical Christianity. In carrying out this mission, CRI's strategy is expressed by the acronym *E-Q-U-I-P:*

The "E" in EQUIP represents the word *essentials.* CRI is committed to the maxim: "In essentials unity, in nonessentials liberty, and in all things charity.

The "Q" in the acronym EQUIP represents the word *questions.* In addition to focusing on essentials, CRI answers people's questions regarding cults, culture, and Christianity.

The "U" in the word EQUIP represents the word *user-friendly.* As much as possible, CRI is committed to taking complex issues and making them understandable and accessible to the lay Christian.

This brings us to the "I" in EQUIP, which stands for *integrity.* Recall Paul's admonition: "Watch your life and doctrine closely. Persevere in them, because if you do, you will save both yourself and your hearers."

Finally, the "P" in the acronym EQUIP represents the word *para-church.* CRI is deeply committed to the local church as the God-ordained vehicle for equipping, evangelism, and education.

Contact Christian Research Institute:

By Mail:
CRI United States
P.O. Box 8500
Charlotte, NC 28271-8500

In Canada:
CRI Canada
56051 Airways P.O.
Calgary, Alberta T2E 8K5

By Phone:
24-hour Customer Service (U.S.)
  (704) 887-8200
24-hour Toll-Free Credit Card Line 1
  (888) 7000-CRI
Fax (704) 887-8299

For information (Canada)
  (403) 571-6363
24-Hour Toll-Free Customer Service
  (Canada)
1 (800) 665-5851
  (orders and donations only)

On the Internet:
www.equip.org

On the Broadcast:
To contact the *Bible Answer Man* broadcast with your questions, call toll free in the U.S. and Canada, 1 (888) ASK HANK (275-4265), Monday–Friday, 5:50 P.M. to 7:00 P.M. Eastern Time.

For a list of stations airing the *Bible Answer Man* or to listen to the broadcast via the Internet, log onto our Web site at www.equip.org.